D1307520

CONTROL
FREAKS

GERALD W. PIAGET, Ph.D

PRODUCED BY THE PHILIP LIEF GROUP, INC.

CONTROL FREAKS

WHO THEY ARE AND HOW TO STOP THEM FROM RUNNING YOUR LIFE

DOUBLEDAY

NEW YORK   LONDON   TORONTO   SYDNEY   AUCKLAND

PUBLISHED BY DOUBLEDAY
a division of Bantam Doubleday Dell Publishing Group, Inc.
666 Fifth Avenue, New York, New York 10103

DOUBLEDAY and the portrayal of an anchor with a dolphin
are trademarks of Doubleday, a division of Bantam Doubleday
Dell Publishing Group, Inc.

Book design by Patrice Fodero

LIBRARY OF CONGRESS CATALOGING-IN-PUBLICATION DATA
Piaget, Gerald W.
Control freaks : who they are and how to stop
them from running your life / Gerald W. Piaget ;
produced by the Philip Lief Group, Inc.
p.   cm.
Includes index.
1. Control (Psychology)   2. Assertiveness training.
3. Aikido—Philosophy. I. Philip Lief Group.
II. Title.
BF611.P63   1991
155.2'32—dc20   90-26387
                                               CIP

ISBN 0-385-41279-7

Copyright © 1991 by Gerald W. Piaget, Ph.D., and the Philip Lief Group, Inc.
All Rights Reserved
Printed in the United States of America
July 1991

1   3   5   7   9   10   8   6   4   2

First Edition

To Craig and Ryan
who have taught me
so many things
I thought I already knew

ACKNOWLEDGMENTS

First and foremost, to Joan, for her love, her help, her understanding, and mainly for putting up with it all. She generated ideas, edited, wrote, typed, made coffee, critiqued, supported, rescheduled, baby-sat, and no matter how grumpy I got, never once threw me off the porch. To Ryan and Craig, who pretty much went without a father during the Killer Month. And then the next Killer Month. You guys make it worthwhile.

Special thanks go to Janet Wells, who came all the way from Australia to help. How did you know? To Errol Schubot, for his ideas, his support, and his love, both now and through the years. There are very few magicians in the world, but Errol is one of them. To Nancy Kalish, who started it all—I hope some day we actually get to work together. And to the people at Doubleday and the Philip Lief Group: Casey Fuetsch, Philip Lief, Susan Meltzner, Susan Moldow, and Lisa Schwartzburg.

Finally, warm thanks to everyone who agreed to submit to a "control freak interview." This book couldn't have been written without your stories, insights and reactions, and the little pieces of your lives you contributed over bland lunches, cold coffee or nothing at all. Thanks also for sharing your control freaks; I hope I represented them fairly. And to the thousands of seminar participants down through the years who instructed me even as I instructed them. Ultimately, the ideas in this book are yours, not mine.

As always, to Grace. I wish you were here.

Gerald W. Piaget
Portola Valley, California
December 20, 1990

CONTENTS

INTRODUCTION
HOLDING WITH AN OPEN HAND

Once upon a time, a boy found a sparrow with a broken wing in the woods outside his home. He took the bird inside, made a cage for it out of sticks, and patiently nursed it back to health. It wasn't long before he came to love the little creature and began to think of it as "his."

Within a month or so the bird's wing had healed. Soon, it began to try to escape from its cage, flapping its wings and hurling itself against the bars. Seeing this, the boy's father said, "Son, you have to let her go. She is a wild thing, and could never be happy in a cage. If you keep her, she will only hurt herself, and may try to hurt you as well."

They carried the cage outside, and the boy gently lifted the sparrow out. Sensing freedom, the bird spread its wings and tried to fly. Reflexively, the boy closed his hand, suddenly afraid of losing his pet forever. The bird squawked and flapped.

"My son," said the father softly, "open your hand. I know you love her, but see how she struggles. In a moment her fragile wings may break. If you squeeze her tightly enough to prevent her escape, you will hurt her, maybe even kill her."

"But if I open my hand, she'll fly away!" cried the boy.

"Maybe so," answered the father. "On the other hand, if she flies, someday she may return. But if your fear of losing her causes you to cripple or kill her, you'll lose her for sure. *The only way one can ever hold something wild and free is with an open hand.*"

So the boy opened his hand, and of course the sparrow immediately flew away. He sadly watched it go, then he and his father went back inside. All that day he felt a terrible loneliness. But the next morning he awoke to the familiar sound of chirping and saw a little sparrow sitting on a branch outside his window. The boy didn't know if it was *his* sparrow or not, but as he went down to breakfast he realized the loneliness was gone.

The foregoing is my version of an ancient Japanese fable which I have come to find quite meaningful. What a hard choice that boy had to make! And how similar it is to choices that we all face in our own lives. Maintaining the proper balance between controlling and letting go is a difficult and never-ending struggle. And the ability to use that elusive, almost paradoxical, third alternative—holding with an open hand—takes courage and faith as well as skill.

Control Freaks

The term "control freak" is a street idiom of fairly recent vintage, the meaning and implications of which seem to vary from one speaker and one situation to another. Among other things, most people consider the label disparaging only when it is applied to *someone else.* If George calls Fred a control freak, it is nearly always a criticism. The implication is that Fred is a pushy, self-centered egomaniac who comes on like a bull in a china shop. He may get results, but he doesn't have the skill or finesse to get things done in a more laid-back manner, and in general he isn't particularly pleasant to be around. But, when George calls *himself* a control freak, the implications are much less negative. In many cases, the admission comes flavored with more than a hint of pride. "Well, maybe I shouldn't be so controlling—I'll try to lighten up. I guess I do come on a little strong sometimes. But I get things done, don't I? And I don't take crap from anyone!"

Of course, some major-league control freaks have no ambivalence at all—they come right out and brag about it. According to Woodward and Bernstein in *All the President's Men,* during his tenure at the White House G. Gordon Liddy had a little sign on his desk that read, "When you've got them by the balls, their hearts and minds will follow."

INTRODUCTION

As it is used in this book, the term "control freak" is in no way derogatory. It is *descriptive.* It refers to someone who consistently controls too much or at the wrong times—someone who needs to be in charge, who can't let go. In other words, someone who can't hold with an open hand when it is necessary or preferable to do so.

Actually, most of us can turn into control freaks under the right circumstances. Some of us hide it better than others, and others use tactics which are so passive, indirect or elegantly subtle that they aren't recognized for what they are. But, at one time or another, almost all of us have let our control needs get the better of us. I certainly have—as a matter of fact, that is one of the main reasons I wrote this book. In the last twenty years I've learned a bit about how to deal with my own control needs; but for a good portion of my life, I was a runaway, card-carrying control freak.

During most of my adolescence and young adulthood, I could not back down in an argument or avoid a fistfight without feeling terrible about it —and making a mental note to get even at some point in the future. I played Teacher/Student (see page 91) with all my girlfriends, reveling in the power and ego boost that gambit *temporarily* provided—and, of course, gradually destroying each relationship in the process.

Showing feelings was fine—if I showed them in order to reach a particular objective (impressing a woman, winning an argument). Otherwise, forget it. Showing feelings just makes you vulnerable, and I didn't need that. (I now realize I already felt so incredibly vulnerable in so many areas that I could never do anything that might make me feel even more so.)

Of course, I knew that in some ways things weren't going very well, but I never really got a handle on what was wrong until, in my late twenties, I became interested in the martial art of *aikido.* Then I began to see that there *were* alternatives to giving in or fighting back, controlling or being controlled. Amazingly, I learned that yielding could be a more powerful tactic than fighting, especially in the long run—and that it was certainly nothing to be ashamed of! Gradually, I began to learn how to hold with an open hand.

Though I haven't studied aikido formally in years, I still practice its teachings, which I find come as close to my personal "truth" as anything I've experienced, as a psychologist or as a human being. I certainly haven't mastered the "open hand" business yet—far from it. That is a lifelong quest for almost anyone. But I believe I'm closer than when I began. Later in this book you will learn a bit about aikido, and how you may be able to apply some of its principles in your own life.

About the Book

The material in this book is drawn from my professional experience as a therapist and trainer, my personal experience with other control-oriented people, more than twenty-five years of immersion in the self-help and training literature, and from a series of in-depth interviews with men and women of different ages, racial and cultural backgrounds, and walks of life. The stories and examples are based on the lives of real people. However, all names and identifying facts have been changed; and in the interest of both confidentiality and succinctness, in some cases information about several individuals was compiled into one composite characterization.

Any self-help book must be written from a particular perspective and must be intended for a particular audience. This one is aimed primarily at helping people deal more effectively with the control freaks in their lives. However, if like me you happen to *be* a control freak, there may be something here for you as well. Maybe your spouse or lover or some other significant person lent you this book, suggesting that you might find someone in it you recognize. Maybe you received four or five copies for your birthday (what a coincidence). Go ahead, open it up, take a look. What have you got to lose? You might learn something. At the very least, you'll get some idea of the new tactics and strategies your significant other may soon be using to deal with *you.*

Whatever your objectives may be, this book addresses the issues, serves the needs, and satisfies whatever curiosities may have led you to open it in the first place. I hope you enjoy reading it, and if you decide to implement some of what it suggests, I wish you the very best of luck.

PART ONE

CONTROL FREAKS

1

CONTROL FREAKS AND ACCOMMODATORS
AN OVERVIEW

"Oh yeah. I know someone like that." With a chuckle or a groan, an emphatic nod or an exasperated grimace, colleagues, clients and friends uttered these words as soon as they heard this was to be a book about control freaks. Even those who had never heard the term before instinctively recognized it and proceeded to describe people in their own lives who fit the bill. As their tales of meddling managers, sulking spouses, pushy parents, manipulative lovers and intimidating co-workers unfolded, it became apparent that the term "control freak" did not just strike a familiar chord, it hit a nerve. Here are just three of the many examples they described.

The Bully

"Write a chapter about my father-in-law," said Drew, a thirty-three-year-old emergency room physician. "He'd love it!" Drew's outrage came through loud and clear as he elaborated. "Carl's the most arrogant, opinionated, dictatorial man I've ever met. 'Father Knows Best' on a power trip. He thinks he knows what's best for everyone. Never lets you forget it. Never lets up. When it comes to sheer pigheadedness, he's in a class by himself."

For years, Carl had been implying that his daughter would be happier if Drew made more money and treated a better class of patients. Recently, Drew had learned that Carl had pulled some strings to get him an interview with a prestigious medical group. "Carl knew I wasn't interested in joining that practice," Drew seethed. "But he's incapable of taking no for an answer."

According to Drew, Carl was so aggressive that he would overhear total strangers ordering in a restaurant and butt in to inform them that they'd be sorry and should choose something else. "He just can't resist telling other people what to do," Drew explained. "He'll interrupt any conversation to correct someone's grammar. I've seen him snatch a cigarette out of someone's hand, put it out and launch into a ten-minute lecture on the evils of smoking—even though he was a guest in that person's home at the time. That's how pushy he is."

The proverbial self-made man, Carl's pushiness had worked to his advantage in classrooms, on playing fields and during his rise from insurance salesman to president of his own corporation. With nothing—no matter how small—escaping his ever watchful eye, Carl rarely missed an opportunity to demonstrate how smart, supercompetent and powerful he was. If he spotted a spelling error in a memo or report, he did not merely point it out to the employee who made it. He brought a dictionary to the culprit's desk and stood there while the employee looked up the misspelled word. For days afterward, whenever he saw that individual, Carl would administer a pop quiz, demanding that the employee spell the word right there and then, sometimes with dozens of other staff members watching. "He brags about stuff like that," Drew commented. "It never occurs to him that he might be humiliating that employee or embarrassing himself by making such a big deal over nothing."

As overbearing as Carl could be in social and business settings, his most tyrannical behavior seemed to be reserved for his family. Although his children—three sons and the daughter to whom Drew was married—no longer lived under his roof, Carl continued to meddle intrusively in their lives. "A few years back, my wife's brother, Billy, was dating a perfectly nice woman," Drew recalled. "But Carl couldn't stand her. He was convinced that because she happened to be divorced and had a young child, she was looking for a free ride—you know, someone to support her and her kid." Carl told Billy to drop the woman and when he didn't, Carl forbade him to bring her to any family functions. "If he heard one of us ask Billy about her, he flipped," Drew continued. "He didn't want 'that gold digger'

4

discussed in his presence. 'That gold digger' was what he always called her. He refused to refer to her by name."

When the relationship fell apart, Carl, oblivious to his son's misery, was elated and took full credit for the relationship's demise. "Didn't I say that girl was no good?" he gloated. "Next time you'll listen to me when I tell you what's right."

You may not have anyone as domineering as Carl in your life right now, but you have probably encountered people like him. Placing themselves at the center of the universe, they have such a strong sense of their own self-importance and superiority that they act as if they have a right to call the shots in any and all situations. No one can understand or handle things as well as I can, they think—and believe that their businesses, families and possibly civilization itself would cease to exist if they were not available to give unsolicited advice, deliver lectures on proper conduct and mete out punishment for various misdeeds.

Of course, not everyone who goes overboard trying to influence what you think, feel or do is as confident as Carl. In fact, some of the most controlling individuals in your life may be extremely insecure.

5

The Worrywart

"My boss is a world-class worrywart," twenty-seven-year-old Kelly, a public relations assistant, claimed. "She leaves nothing to chance." Irene, public relations director for a nationwide chain of department stores, spent at least twenty minutes going over every detail each time she gave Kelly an assignment. "I may have done the same exact job a hundred times," Kelly said, "but she'll explain it to me as if it was my first day on the job. Then, maybe ten minutes later, she'll call—just to make sure I understood some point that a trained chimpanzee could understand. Before the project's completed, I'll get at least ten more of those 'just checking' calls—and that's for a minor project."

For *major* projects, Irene consulted half a dozen people and told Kelly what they said in addition to what she thought. "Then, every morning, we'll play Twenty Questions," Kelly continued, her frustration becoming more and more apparent. "She wants to know where things stand on the project, what part of it I'm working on that day, if I'd forgotten anything and on and on. Sometimes I feel like shaking her and shouting, 'Stop treating me like an idiot! I can do the damn assignment and I'd do it a whole lot faster if you'd just leave me alone!' "

When Kelly wasn't fantasizing about wringing Irene's neck, she was doubting her own competence and questioning her own sanity. "I used to think there was something wrong with me," Kelly said, "that Irene treated me like a ditz because I acted like I was one or that I had a problem with authority figures or something." But then she realized that Irene hovered over the rest of the public relations staff too. "She had to know what everyone was doing every minute of the day," Kelly continued. "She'd even play these little games where she told one of us that she was worried about something someone else was doing. She'd ask us to keep an eye on that person and to let her know what was going on. Pretty soon we were all spying on each other, which didn't do much for our morale."

Irene played other games as well, setting up competitions between her staff and the advertising department, or playing on people's insecurities and getting more work out of them by telling them what *she* had been able to accomplish when *she* was in their position. "Sometimes she flat-out lied," Kelly claimed. "She'd tell us that *her* boss insisted something had to be done a certain way or by a certain time. But it would be her idea all along and her boss wouldn't even know about it. Honestly, that woman would do *anything* to keep us in line or, as she put it, to keep us from screwing things up for her."

As exasperating as Carl was infuriating, people like Irene nag, check up on you and bombard you with questions and reminders because they are afraid of what might happen if they did not. They seem afraid that if they let one little detail get by them or if they loosen their grip for even an instant, they will lose control over the entire situation, fall apart at the seams, get fired or suffer any number of other horrifying fates. Apt to be perfectionists or people who have overcome adversity, handicaps or discrimination, these overly cautious controllers can often be found among managers and executives whose climb up the career ladder involved setting goals and using everything within their power to reach them. Over the years, they got into the habit of controlling in order to get what they wanted and became almost superstitious about operating in any other way. One slipup and I could lose everything I've gained, they think, and control just to make sure nothing goes wrong. As anyone who has ever been involved with or observed an overprotective parent, insecure lover or overcommitted, stressed-out neighbor knows, this attitude and approach are not restricted to business settings.

The Takeover Artist

Beverly, a housewife in her midfifties, had lived next door to Ellen for nearly twenty years and, even though the two women were friends and frequently did things together, Beverly claimed that she had never understood Ellen and probably never would.

According to Beverly, Ellen was very particular about everything from how her clothes hung in her closet to how the hedges in her yard were trimmed. Every minute of her day was scheduled in advance and nothing less than a natural disaster could get her to change her plans. "I used to call that being finicky," Beverly said. "I figured that she had a right to live her life that way if she wanted to." The trouble was that Ellen tried to make other people live their lives her way too.

"No matter where she is, Ellen takes over," Beverly continued. "She'll come into your kitchen and straighten your cabinets. You'll look out your window and see her weeding your garden. She'll decide that you need a new sweatsuit or a different brand of shampoo, buy it for you without asking, bring it over and expect you to pay for it. Sometimes she'll go right into your wallet and take the money you 'owe' her."

Once Ellen got an idea into her head, she wouldn't let go of it.

The previous Sunday was a perfect example. At eight in the morning, Beverly had received a "frantic" call from Ellen. She and her husband were going to the movies that afternoon and needed to check the theater schedule but couldn't because the entertainment section was missing from their newspaper. She wanted to borrow Beverly's and Beverly, who was still in bed, agreed to bring it over in an hour or so.

"But she wanted it right that instant," Beverly recalled. "She got really worked up about it and kept listing everything she planned to do in the order she planned to do it—as if that justified getting me out of bed. It didn't even make any sense. I mean, the first showing of *any* movie was hours away and it was going to take her all of one minute to look up the listings. What difference did it make if she did it right then or an hour later?"

Although Beverly generally went along with anything Ellen asked her to do, this time she stood firm, informing Ellen that she would bring the entertainment section over in an hour and not a moment sooner. "I thought that was that," Beverly continued. "But the next thing I knew, Ellen was knocking on the door. Since I wouldn't bring the paper to her, she'd decided to come and get it herself."

Control Freaks

People like Carl, Irene and Ellen are "control freaks": people who control too much, too often or when control is not actually required. Some nag, threaten, filibuster or intimidate, leaving little doubt about their intentions. Others control covertly, drawing upon a truly ingenious talent for manipulation. Their double binds, mixed messages and deceptions can be so subtle that you don't even realize you are being manipulated until after the fact. All seem bound and determined to get their own way no matter what and appear to be more than willing to sacrifice your happiness and peace of mind in order to maintain their own.

Extreme controlling behavior is baffling at best. Interacting with a control freak can leave you feeling angry, frustrated, resentful or victimized. Nothing seems to stop them. Running into brick walls does not deter them. The fact that they are riding roughshod over people—including people they love—does not dissuade them. They MUST compel you to go along with their game plan. They MUST get you to agree with them or get you out of their way. It is not a matter of choice for most control freaks. They operate out of habit rather than preference or necessity and feel successful, secure, worthwhile or at ease if—and only if—they are calling the shots.

Even milder control tactics can frustrate you and wear you down after a while. Life with a controller begins to feel like a never-ending contest. You must be constantly on guard for the cutting remark, the subtle criticism, the undermining look. You must be ever watchful of the friend or spouse who is always looking for ways to take just a little more than his or her share.

And no matter how hard you try, you won't catch them all. Truly skillful control freaks can be *hours* into a maneuver before you even notice that something is wrong—and you notice then only because you feel tired and your stomach has begun to hurt.

QUESTIONNAIRE—RECOGNIZING CONTROL FREAKS

Is there a control freak in your life? Pick someone you think might fit that label. Now, take a minute to assess the following statements. The results will indicate the extent to which you feel there are people around who do try to control you.

Rate each of the following items on a 5-point scale. A 5 indicates that the item is *very* descritive of the person you picked; a 1 means the item is not at all descriptive of that person.

Item	Not Descriptive				Very Descriptive
1. Winning an argument seems more important to him/her than coming up with the best solution.	1	2	3	4	5
2. S/he tends to get angry or impatient in a traffic jam.	1	2	3	4	5
3. When I don't do what s/he wants, s/he gets angry, pouts or gives me the silent treatment.	1	2	3	4	5
4. It's important to her/him that other people think s/he is in charge.	1	2	3	4	5
5. I often keep my opinions to myself because it isn't	1	2	3	4	5

Item	Not Descriptive		Very Descriptive		

worth the hassle to disagree.

Item	Not		Very		
6. Driving in a strange town, s/he would rather get lost than ask for directions.	1	2	3	4	5
7. S/he does favors for me without my asking, and would feel offended if I asked her/him not to.	1	2	3	4	5
8. We have arguments about small things that wind up ruining the evening.	1	2	3	4	5
9. S/he seems happiest when bossing people around.	1	2	3	4	5
10. S/he is much better at giving orders than at taking them.	1	2	3	4	5
11. S/he always seems to be into other peoples' business.	1	2	3	4	5
12. S/he's always keeping an eye on everyone or every detail to keep things from getting screwed up.	1	2	3	4	5
13. If s/he doesn't like a movie or the food at a restaurant, no one else should either.	1	2	3	4	5
14. We always seem to do what s/he wants.	1	2	3	4	5
15. S/he pouts if s/he's not the center of attention.	1	2	3	4	5

Item	Not Descriptive				Very Descriptive
16. S/he criticizes everyone for being inefficient and unorganized.	1	2	3	4	5
17. S/he gets furious whenever anyone touches anything around her/his desk or office.	1	2	3	4	5
18. S/he delegates *responsibility* but not *authority*. When I do make a decision on my own, s/he criticizes and often overrides it.	1	2	3	4	5
19. S/he gets overly upset when her/his plans fall through or have to be rearranged.	1	2	3	4	5
20. S/he can't stand the idea of messiness or disarray.	1	2	3	4	5

Did any of these items ring a bell with you? If you rated many of them a 4 or 5, or if your score on the survey as a whole is above about 60, you may have a control freak on your hands.

Normal Control

There is nothing wrong with wanting to be in control. We all want to feel in charge of our lives, to have an impact on the world around us, and to believe that we can make our dreams come true. Life would be difficult indeed if everything we wanted and every goal we hoped to achieve were dictated by the winds of fate or other people's whims. The prospect of such utter powerlessness is depressing and, for many of us, terrifying.

Every day of our lives we encounter circumstances that can trigger this natural urge to control. So we take charge, and in many cases are better off for having done so. We carry a young child from the path of an oncoming car to the safety of the sidewalk, not stopping to think whether or not we might be violating the child's rights in the process. In a staff meeting we voice a strong opinion about the creation of a new product line, and do all we can to convince others we are right. Who is *really* right becomes, at least temporarily, less of an issue than who can present the most convincing argument. In short, we control to make our lives as successful, interesting and secure as possible, and to aid those around us when and as we can.

Of course, sometimes we go overboard. We plan, scheme, manipulate—and act in ways we later regret. Sometimes we try too hard, not recognizing we've reached the point of diminishing returns. Relentlessly trying to wedge a square peg into a round hole, we may appear foolish or obsessed, hurt people we love, and, hell-bent on having it our own way, wind up with nothing.

But for most of us, going so far overboard tends to be the exception rather than the rule. When it finally dawns on us that our control needs may actually be making matters worse, we generally stop trying to control and look for another way to proceed. We may lay our cards on the table and try for a negotiated compromise, withdraw, saving our energies for other battles, or table the issue at hand, giving our differences a chance to settle. This is what sets us "normal controllers" apart from control freaks. Everyone has the urge to control, and in truth, there may be a bit of the control freak in most of us. But most of us can turn it off.

Control Addicts

Control freaks can't stop. They are, in essence, control addicts. They have *lost control of their urge to control* in much the same way other addicts lose control over their need for alcohol, drugs, food or sex. At any cost and regardless of the consequences, control freaks will strive to satisfy their intense, ever present craving for control (or the illusion of control). It simply never dawns on them that their incessant controlling may be causing more harm than good.

Unfortunately, there really are some mean-spirited, abusive people in this world—people whose aim is to hurt you, make you dependent on them or prevent you from thinking for yourself. But most control freaks are neither evil nor mentally ill. Driven by needs that they may not even be aware of, they are simply incapable of operating in any other way. This does not excuse their behavior or justify the damage they may do. But it does not make them inherently bad people either. Furthermore, they may often be useful—or fun—to have around.

The people who pull your strings and push your buttons can also charm and delight you. They can be articulate and amusing, smart and successful. During a crisis, you may actually be grateful for that "take charge" approach of theirs.

Many extremely successful individuals call themselves control freaks and do so with pride. They are convinced that they would not be where they are today if they had operated in any other way—and they may be right. We admire, respect and perhaps even wish that we were more like these people who take the bull by the horns, know exactly what they want, go after it, and let nothing stand in their way.

13

Many controllers go to extremes only occasionally, or under certain circumstances. They might, for instance, overcontrol in the workplace and be pussycats at home—or push their spouses around but be pushovers with their kids. If they are in leadership positions, power may go to their heads. Yet, when they are simply committee or team members, they seem perfectly content to follow someone else's lead. Stressful situations can also trigger control-freak behavior in certain individuals. Sick children, upcoming visits from highly critical in-laws, the prospect of coordinating a large conference, or the simple fear of losing an important relationship have all pushed more than one closet control freak over the edge.

Still, when people in your own life are hell-bent on getting you to see or do things their way or when you get caught in the crossfire of their efforts to control everything around them, it is difficult not to cast them as villains. *They* are making my life miserable, you think. *They* leave me no choices, invade my privacy, steamroll right over me. Because of *them* I can't do my job or feel good about myself. Having come to those conclusions, it is easy to assume that *they* must be the undisputed bad guys and that *they* must change their ways before your life can improve. However, *they* are only part of the problem.

Accommodation

It is time to take a look at how you respond to the control freaks in your lives. Please take a minute to complete the questionnaire in the accompanying box.

EVALUATING THE TENDENCY TO ACCOMMODATE

Each of the following items ends the sentence "When someone tries to control me, or asks me to do something I don't want to do, I ———.''

Rate each item on a 5-point scale. A 5 indicates the item is *very* descriptive of you; a 1 means the item is not at all descriptive of you.

Response	Not Descriptive				Very Descriptive
1. generally go along, because it isn't worth the hassle to do otherwise.	1	2	3	4	5
2. sometimes say yes because I fear the consequences of saying no.	1	2	3	4	5
3. take a stand and refuse or fight back, no matter what the consequences.	1	2	3	4	5
4. try to clown or sweet-talk my way out of doing what they want.	1	2	3	4	5
5. get angry and give them a piece of my mind.	1	2	3	4	5

	Response	Not Descriptive			Very Descriptive	
6.	agree to the request, but then "forget" to follow through.	1	2	3	4	5
7.	agree and follow through, but then complain about it afterward.	1	2	3	4	5
8.	fight fire with fire— make some requests or demands of my own.	1	2	3	4	5
9.	allow myself to be controlled, but then get back at them later.	1	2	3	4	5
10.	fight back at first, but eventually get worn down and give in.	1	2	3	4	5
11.	pout or sulk.	1	2	3	4	5
12.	often comply because I think I should, and would feel bad if I did anything else.	1	2	3	4	5
13.	fight back and feel guilty afterward.	1	2	3	4	5
14.	give in, then feel angry at myself for being weak.	1	2	3	4	5

If you answered 4 or 5 to many of the questionnaire items, or if your total score is above 40, the next few pages may be particularly relevant for you. Pay attention to the specific items you rated 3 or higher. Some people naturally tend to give in to controlling behavior, some automatically fight back against it, and some respond indirectly, or do a little bit of both. There are times when some of these responses may be appropriate, or the best alternative available. But if you respond *consistently* in this fashion, you may be doing your cause more harm than good.

Giving In and Fighting Back

Let's return for a moment to two of the accommodators you met at the beginning of this chapter.

"What do I do when Ellen orders me around?" Beverly said, repeating the question I had asked her. "What do you think? I do whatever she wants me to do. I get so rattled that it never occurs to me to do anything else."

Minutes or hours after their interaction, Beverly would berate herself for "being so dumb and caving in" to Ellen's demands. But at the moment Ellen made those demands, Beverly almost always complied. She gave in immediately and as if she had no other choice.

Even more disconcerting to Beverly was the time and energy she devoted to anticipating Ellen's next move. She walked on eggs in Ellen's presence, carefully choosing every word she uttered. "And there's plenty of things I just don't tell her because I know she'll yell at me," Beverly explained. Constantly watching her step, Beverly considered Ellen's probable reaction before making decisions or taking actions of her own. Miserably, she confessed that on more than one occasion she'd actually found herself staring into her clothes closet, choosing what to wear based on whether or not Ellen would approve.

Drew, on the other hand, flatly refused to play the game by Carl's rules. As far as he was concerned, "If you gave Carl an inch, he'd take a mile. If you did it his way once, the next thing you know he'd be running your entire life." With that premise firmly planted in his mind, Drew resisted Carl's each and every move. He went out of his way *not* to follow Carl's advice and disregarded any suggestions Carl offered—even the ones that were relatively reasonable and actually could have proven useful to him.

As you might expect, Carl and Drew's relationship was far from peaceful. "We've had some real knock-down drag-out fights over the years," Drew admitted. "And we'll probably have plenty more."

Two Sides of the Same Coin

Although they appear to be very different, Beverly's and Drew's reactions to the control freaks in their lives were quite similar in a number of ways. For one thing, both were *automatic reactions rather than consciously chosen courses of action.* Neither Beverly nor Drew seriously considered other options or, with forethought, decided to comply or resist. They just did it. In fact, Beverly sometimes gave in so quickly and instinctively that she did not realize she had done so until later on.

Secondly, for both, *avoiding a particular outcome seemed to take precedence over dealing effectively with the situation at hand.* Beverly complied with demands that were downright ridiculous because she was more concerned with not being yelled at or criticized than with doing what was in her own best interest. Drew was so determined not to let Carl tell him what to do that he did not pay attention to the actual advice Carl was offering or attempt to differentiate between intrusive, inappropriate meddling and sound, potentially beneficial suggestions.

Finally, by responding in the way they did, both Beverly and Drew *encouraged the overly controlling individuals in their lives to try again or try harder to control them.* Each time Beverly gave in, and especially when she did what she guessed Ellen wanted before Ellen even made a move, Beverly was essentially saying, "Here, go ahead. Walk all over me. I'll even show you where to step and although I may complain about you to other people, I will never tell *you* how much I resent what you're doing." Obviously, Ellen wasn't about to turn down such a gracious invitation to do what she wanted to do in the first place. And, if you think Drew had it any better, you'll have to think again. Rarely did fighting back get Carl to back off. Indeed, Drew's blatant resistance only made Carl more resolute and he employed ever more ingenious—and infuriating—control tactics to convince his son-in-law to see and do things his way.

Even though their individual actions were quite different, Beverly and Drew were actually using variations on the same response pattern. They were *accommodating,* and if you routinely get taken in, sidetracked, bowled over or immobilized by someone else's controlling behavior, you are probably doing it too.

Accommodating as a Way of Life

Most of us accommodate control freaks almost without knowing it. We don't realize that we are letting someone else's behavior dictate our own or that we are giving that person the power to control us. We may think we are making an even trade, getting something that seems more important to us than calling the shots or being in charge.

Sometimes we don't know what else to do or, like Beverly, we get so rattled that other options simply never occur to us. We respond in ways that are familiar and comfortable, engaging in behaviors that worked to our advantage in the past and still feel like the right thing to do. Trying to make other people happy and trying to avoid conflicts are two responses that, when done to excess, make us prime targets for anyone with a powerful urge to push people around.

Ironically, so does a natural inclination to resist. When you arbitrarily fight back, or when you comply but then devote yourself to getting even, you are still allowing the other person's behavior to control yours. You are still putting your goals and priorities aside as you apply yourself to keeping the control freak from achieving his or hers.

Accommodating behavior is automatic, and usually the same patterns are repeated over and over again. Frequently you are convinced that your way will work if only you try hard enough to make it work. And so you try harder and harder, behaving in the same manner repeatedly despite dismal results and unhealthy consequences. Eventually you may get hooked on your ineffective response patterns, and develop an accommodating habit over which you have little or no control. Just as with the control freak in your life, what you are doing does not accomplish what you hoped it would accomplish and often makes matters worse, *but you cannot seem to stop.*

Whether you

- comply too easily and too often, giving up too much and getting little more in return than ulcers, anxiety and more demands for compliance

- resist too quickly and too globally, cutting off your nose to spite your face in your haste to guarantee that no one gets the better of you

- play the perennial victim and get caught up with control freaks in various settings
- or perpetually rebel, rabble-rouse, connive or seek revenge, guaranteeing that most if not all of your relationships are rife with conflict

your accommodating habit can do as much to defeat you as anything a control freak does to you. Furthermore, the combined effect of someone else's automatic, habitual efforts to control you and your automatic, habitual response to those efforts can create vicious cycles of moves and countermoves known as "control traps."

Control Traps

We've all seen variations on the following theme. A toddler riding in his mother's shopping cart at the supermarket struggles to his feet. His mother gently sits him down again, saying, "No, honey. It's dangerous to stand up. You might fall." Little Richie yells, "NO! OUT!" and once more tries to stand. Mommy sits him down again, and hands him her keys. "Here, Richie, play with these while you ride," she says. Richie drops the keys, stands up, and begins to climb out of the cart.

Mommy sits him down and whispers angrily, "No, you can't get out! Now please keep quiet!" Little Richie begins to cry, and tries to stand. Mommy grabs his arm and sits him down again; her son responds by crying even harder.

When Mommy turns away, Richie throws a large container of raspberry yogurt out of the cart. The splat of yogurt hitting linoleum gets the attention of any shoppers who have not already been drawn into our little drama. Mommy gasps, slaps Richie's hand, and snarl-whispers, "Just wait till I get you home, young man. I'll give you something to cry about!" Richie bellows. At this point, his mother looks up with embarrassment at the other shoppers, realizing she's managed to create just the scene she'd so much wanted to avoid. She mumbles something unintelligible, grabs her screaming child, and leaves the store without her groceries.

Richie is a control freak. (All toddlers are control freaks—it's part of the job description.) His methods, if not particularly pleasant, are straightforward: when he doesn't get what he wants he cries, kicks his feet, flops around, maybe throws some yogurt. And he'll keep trying to get his way until he tires or his attention is distracted.

Richie's mother, under normal circumstances, is *not* a control freak. She loves her son a great deal, and she tries to accommodate to his moods and preferences when she can. But in situations when she feels she needs to take a firmer hand, she has a problem. When her efforts at reason and distraction fail at the supermarket, Richie's mother doesn't know what else to do besides using direct physical and verbal force. But Richie rarely receives such treatment at home, and he isn't used to it. Far from controlling his behavior, it makes him feel frightened and upset, and causes him to redouble his efforts.

Mommy is getting upset as well. Her son is making a scene in public, and she has been raised to detest scenes. She knows everyone in the store is watching her—and at that moment it feels as if her very identity as a parent and a human being is on the line. Further, she remembers that this sort of thing happens nearly every time she and Richie go to the grocery store. The feelings of helplessness and frustration that are part of the life of every young mother begin to surface. She tries harder to control Richie, using tactics that at another time she would deplore; he fights back. The efforts of each inflame the other, and at some point they both lose it.

We all recognize these deadly little patterns because we've all experienced them ourselves. At one time or another they've driven most of us nuts. When you badly want to achieve a particular outcome; when everything you try only seems to make things worse; and when, despite the evidence, *you still can't stop trying*—then you are in a control trap. Many of the trapping patterns that develop between control freaks and accommodators are much more subtle and complex than Mommy's encounter with Richie and the yogurt. But the essential ingredients are the same.

In a true control trap, everyone is a victim. Who was the villain and who was the victim in the Little Richie story? We may not agree with the way Richie's mother behaved, and in some cases we may be forced to protect ourselves from people who behave that way. But neither did she wake up Thursday morning, brush her teeth and say to herself, "I think I'll give my kid a hard time at the supermarket this afternoon." She behaved the way she did because, under certain circumstances, she goes on automatic pilot. Richie acted the way he did because he doesn't yet know other ways to express his needs. He and his mother are trapped in a pattern which (for different reasons) they can't control. And they both suffer for it.

What Goes Around . . .

At times the terms "control freak" and "accommodator" can be a little misleading. Please don't get the idea that these are two discrete personality types, irrevocably different from one another and sworn natural enemies. Nothing could be further from the truth. Certainly, there are people among us who are prototypical control freaks—who feel driven to take charge in almost any situation, and who virtually never give in. And there are people who seem ready to accommodate at the drop of an innuendo, anytime, anyplace, and with almost anyone.

21

But for most of us, the situation is more complicated. Almost nobody is all one way, and almost nobody is free of these patterns. Control freaks accommodate, and accommodators control. There seems to be a bit of the accommodator and the control freak in most of us, just waiting to pop out when the right buttons get pushed. Furthermore, under closer examination the very distinction between controlling and accommodating begins to blur around the edges.

Like Drew, when we accommodate we often switch into control mode ourselves. A good deal of accommodating behavior is an attempt either to gain some semblance of control over our own lives, or to beat control freaks at their own game and force them to do things *our* way. In a very real sense, control freaks also accommodate accommodators, giving them the opportunity to people-please, give in, rebel, avoid conflict, or use whatever accommodating style they find most comfortable.

Human interaction can be incredibly confusing. Things sometimes get so complicated that you need a scorecard to tell the players apart. Among other things, this means you should resist the temptation to label your boss or wife or father-in-law a control freak because he or she fits one of the patterns described in the following pages. Instead, learn to recognize and deal more effectively with the particular control *tactics* the individual uses when he or she tries to control you. And learn to recognize and overcome the habits and emotional reactions that make you an easy target when the other person *does* act like a control freak. In other words, get ready to make some changes.

Breaking Free

You do not escape from a control trap by doing what you have always done with more skill or determination. Fighting fire with fire—figuring out what control freaks do and then outdoing them at it—is not the answer either. Neither is finding the perfect method for stopping controllers dead in their tracks. That method does not exist. Although it is important to learn to take certain controlling behaviors a bit less seriously, you will never learn to just ignore someone who tries to overpower or undermine you. And all you do is expend valuable energy when you label, blame, and try to punish control freaks. This book is based on the premise that you will never really be able to break free as long as you *compete* with control freaks for control.

But wait. Be assured that there *is* a great deal you *can* do to reduce the power control freaks have over you and to get more of what you want and need from your interactions with them. Even if the controllers in your life do not change one iota, *you* can change enough to keep them from getting to you as easily, as often, or as thoroughly.

As you read, keep these ideas in mind:

- Each and every one of us—control freaks and accommodators alike—is a determined individual doing what we *learned* to do in order to meet our needs, reach our goals, and feel in control of our own lives.

- We *can* meet our needs without doing so at someone else's expense and have disputes without turning them into us-against-them conflicts.

- We *can* stand up for ourselves without stepping on anyone else and cease being victims without becoming victimizers.

- No matter how powerless we feel we *do* have the power

to change ourselves, our attitudes and our responses to circumstances that have been making us miserable.

- We *can* feel less vulnerable, operate more independently and effectively, and cultivate more cooperative relationships by *learning to collaborate rather than compete and to seek harmony rather than hands-down victory.*

This book will help you put these ideas into action. It will increase your awareness and understanding of both your own and other people's controlling and accommodating behaviors. It will help you increase your options for responding to and coping with people who try to control you. And it will provide specific strategies and solutions to try in your own life.

GOTCHA!

THE PATTERNS AND TACTICS OF CONTROL

Can other people actually control what you think, feel or do? Some experts on human behavior say they cannot, that no one can *make* you do anything you choose not to do (or stop you from doing something you truly want to do). In their opinion, when you hand a thief your wallet because he is holding a gun to your head, you are still making a free choice. You are electing to be robbed rather than shot.

As popular as this idea was during the heyday of encounter groups, it is not the last word on control. Nor is it particularly comforting or useful during real-life experiences with control freaks. When you actually face someone who seemingly will do anything to get his own way, you *feel and act* as if both your choices and your freedom to choose have been taken from you.

"How did I get talked into this?" Jonathan, a computer systems analyst, wondered as he nervously reviewed his note cards. One minute he had been having a friendly conversation with his company's community affairs director and the next minute he was agreeing to deliver a Career Day speech to an auditorium full of high school students. "I never knew what hit me," Jonathan sighed.

Neither did George, a retired restaurateur. He was determined *not* to drop everything and rush to the rescue every time his son—who now ran the family business—called to ask for a favor. But somehow his son always wore him down. "I'll say 'no, no, no,'" George grumbled resentfully, "but the next thing I know, I'm there at the restaurant flipping burgers, washing dishes, running the cash register—doing all the things I didn't want to do anymore after I retired."

Meredith, a department store buyer, was also mystified by her own behavior after running into a fast-talking salesman she had dated once or twice several years ago. "Why on earth did I agree to go out with him tonight?" she asked herself as the salesman walked away. "I have a million things to do and I don't even enjoy his company that much."

And each time Lisa's mother, Emma, called to discuss "some itty bitty detail" of Lisa's wedding plans, the twenty-nine-year-old interior designer swore, "This time I'm *not* going to let her get to me." But less than five minutes later, Lisa could be heard shouting into the telephone receiver, "Damn it. This is *my* wedding and if you don't cut it out I'm calling the whole thing off!" Her threat was an idle one, of course. Before the end of the day (and sometimes before the end of the phone conversation), Lisa, feeling guilty about her outburst, would apologize to her mother and do whatever she had so adamantly resisted doing earlier.

25

What happened here? Why in the world would four intelligent adults suddenly switch to automatic pilot, saying and doing things they didn't want to, and which they would later regret? Why couldn't they just say no? Furthermore, these are not isolated occurrences. Under the right circumstances, Jonathan, George, Meredith and Lisa—and many of us as well—will react like this every time. They, along with many of us, fall victim to the people in their lives who know what buttons to push, know exactly when to push them, and have the power to push them hard. How they go about pushing them is the subject of this chapter.

Control Tactics

In the course of history human beings have evolved a truly amazing number of ways to manipulate one another. The term "control freak" probably brings to mind an aggressive, rather intimidating person who cares more about getting what he wants than what he does to people in the process. But control freaks are not always powermongers, nor are they obnoxious jerks. They can be subtle, often they are insecure. Sometimes they aren't even acting according to a conscious game plan. In fact, some of the least obvious controllers can be the most dangerous: when someone seems weak or hurt or needy, we tend to give in —or we refuse and then feel guilty about it. Either way, we become putty in their hands.

What control freaks have in common is success at manipulating other people. Some of the methods they use are quite direct. Controllers may try to attack you, reason with you, wear you down, intimidate you, or simply command you to do their bidding. But no matter how they proceed, their purpose is clear. They are after something, and they believe controlling you and/or the situation at hand may help them get it. Direct methods tend to leave people feeling *overpowered* by the controller's knowledge, emotional intensity, verbal skill, or simple persistence.

Other tactics are much less obvious and direct; these are used by people who want to conceal the fact that they are trying to control you. Some are so subtle and are applied so skillfully that you never recognize them at all—which is what makes indirect control so effective. Generally, you are left feeling more *undermined* than overpowered; it almost seems as if your own thoughts and feelings have been used against you. Indirect tactics often involve the manipulation of emotions: such controllers make you feel guilty, helpless, or so angry you do something you later regret. In addition, contradictions, implications, ambiguities, and other verbal methods are used to lead your thinking in a direction the controller wants it to go.

Of course, some control maneuvers can leave you feeling overpowered and undermined all at once. Furthermore, control freaks almost never use only one technique at a time. They employ control tactics the way good boxers throw punches—in combinations. And the good ones will keep throwing different combinations at you until they find a few that work. In order to help you recognize certain specific control tactics, most of the examples that follow focus on individual moves. But in the real world, when you are dealing with a flesh-and-blood control freak, it is almost never so simple.

With that in mind, let's take a look at a few of the more common direct and indirect control tactics. As you read through the list, see if you can recognize maneuvers the controlling people in your life tend to use on you. Becoming familiar with the ways in which a control freak manipulates you is the first step toward reducing his or her power to do so.

Direct Control Tactics

Here controllers use anger, stated or implied threats, arguments, insults, criticism or physical force to bend you to their will. Sometimes the force of their personality is enough to do the job. And sometimes they just move in and take over. Controllers use their power and intensity against you; you feel outmatched, without sufficient strength, knowledge or skill to fight back effectively.

Takeover

For all the subtle and devious tactics discussed in this book, the most common way control freaks get control is simply by taking it. Ellen, whom you met in the last chapter, is a good example. They move into a situation the way a marine sergeant moves onto a battlefield, and they ask permission just about as frequently. *Assuming* they have the right, almost the duty, to take over, they command, order, instruct, and do whatever else may be necessary to get into the driver's seat and stay there. They may push you out of the way emotionally or verbally, or talk you into a position you really don't want to be in. Then, later, they are surprised or offended if you make a fuss.

Often the transition into control mode is so rapid and so unexpected that other people are taken by surprise. By the time you realize that you don't like the arrangement, the control freak is so firmly entrenched that it is difficult, or at least embarrassing, to dislodge him.

Sometimes the takeover artist *acts* unaware of how invasive he or she is being. Confidence men use this tactic (among others) to set you up for the "sting" which will leave you poorer but (hopefully) wiser. However, in other cases the controller really is unaware of how the accommodator is feeling. This lack of awareness may actually make their position more powerful.

For instance, Mary Jane was the typical "well-meaning friend." She and Judy were next-door neighbors, and when Judy shattered her leg in a skiing accident it was Mary Jane to the rescue. The good lady just about moved in. She cooked, she cleaned, she did the shopping. And she sat by the side of Judy's bed and talked. For hours. After a while, Judy didn't know what was worse: traction or Mary Jane. When she finally began to ask for some privacy, her protests simply were pushed aside. Judy admits she could have tried harder. But she didn't want to seem ungrateful, and she was overwhelmed by the energy and vitality of this well-meaning, horribly helpful woman. Now, Judy is gradually regaining the use of her leg, and Mary Jane has decided they will take a cruise together during Christmas week. Taking a vacation with Mary Jane is the *last* thing Judy wants to do. But so far, she hasn't been able to tell her friend that the rapidly developing cruise plans don't represent to Judy the fruition of a lifelong dream.

Some takeover tactics can be much less direct. Not long ago, the manager of a small company hired Francine, a temporary office worker, to fill in for the vacationing secretary/office manager. Her contract was for a week and her primary responsibility was to help reduce the typing backlog. Three days into this arrangement it was discovered that, as well as completing a reasonable amount of typing, she had rearranged the office's entire filing system. Apparently Francine was looking for a permanent job and had decided that typing wasn't going to provide her with enough of a showcase.

Now, the files had desperately needed updating and Francine had done an acceptable job. They were in much better shape than they'd been the week before, and Francine's other work apparently hadn't suffered in the process. But she hadn't been told to do the files, and the fact that she had done them was going to cause problems. For one thing, the office system index was kept on computer disk and now would have to be updated, a task that would take many hours. For another, the permanent office manager would be back Monday. A territorial and rather insecure individual, it was a good bet she would not be pleased.

When Francine was confronted with the problem, she became angry and defensive. "Don't you like the job I did?" she kept asking. She simply couldn't understand that the issue had little to do with the quality of her filing. Finally she demanded that the manager sign her time card, and left in a huff. (Ironically, if she could have discussed the matter more rationally and admitted she'd overstepped her responsibilities, the manager probably would have offered her a job.)

Assault

An assault is a verbal, emotional, or physical attack. Direct assault is both straightforward and easily recognized; if you are prepared, it can be usually one of the easiest forms of control to deal with. Unless, of course, circumstances make you vulnerable to the kind of assault being used. An inner city teenager walking alone in a rival gang's neighborhood is vulnerable to physical assault, as is the battered woman who can't or won't leave her assaultive husband. If anger, criticism, or the threat of violence frightens you, you may be vulnerable to verbal and emotional attack. Assault is also effective against someone who needs something from the controller, or when used in situations where the controller already has some leverage.

Sam, a free-lance photographer who relies heavily on work subcontracted to him by a small marketing company, provides a good example. Referring to the company president, Sam said, "Cassie gave me my first major assignment. At the time, I was still substitute teaching and bartending to make ends meet. And over the years, she pretty much kept me afloat. Every time I was ready to pack it in and take a straight nine-to-five job, she came through for me. So I really do owe her a lot."

Unfortunately, Cassie had a habit of overextending her staff, and Sam kept getting caught in the crunch. In fact, he had encountered so many problems with Cassie's clients lately that, despite his loyalty and the sense of security her steady assignments gave him, he had begun to wonder if working for her was worth the aggravation. Consequently, when she told him about a "sensational" project she had going and said she wanted him to coordinate portions of it, Sam thanked her but then hedged. He said he would want some assurances that the project would start by a certain date, and asked that Cassie provide a list of objectives for which he would be responsible. Cassie listened to about three sentences, and then exploded.

"I don't believe you!!!" she screamed. "After all I've done for you? How DARE you ask for written guarantees!" Cassie called Sam a "hysterical prima donna" who saw imaginary problems around every bend. She called him ungrateful, accused him of trying to squeeze more money out of her, and repeatedly reminded him that she paid him more than any of her other free-lancers. Finally she slammed her fist onto the desk, and

29

screeched, "So if you're not happy with the assignments I give you, you can WALK!"

Sam was flabbergasted. "I was so stunned that when I could get a word in edgewise, the first thing I did was apologize for upsetting her—even though I had no idea what I might have said or done to do that. She just came off the wall at me!" Once Cassie calmed down, Sam, still in a state of shock, agreed to take her assignment—without any of the assurances or descriptions he wanted. In fact, he never brought them up for discussion again.

Your assailants—the people who try to get the upper hand by knocking you out of the ring—may throw tantrums in situations that thwart or threaten them, using angry tirades as weapons against you. They may blast you, attacking your character and running through a long list of your failings as a human being. They may annihilate you, wiping you out and leaving you defenseless with their intense, unpredictable explosions.

Besides anger, effective assault tactics include criticism and ridicule, showing contempt for you and making caustic comments or jokes at your expense. It really makes no difference whether your husband shouts insults at you or whether he turns to a third party and says, "Well, I never claimed to have married a rocket scientist"—whether your associate calls you every name in the book while furiously pounding on her desk or calmly hands back a report and asks, "Are you really as stupid as this makes you look?" You are still being attacked.

Intimidation

Intimidation is how control freaks control you after they've established their reputations. Intimidators rely on physical assault, tantrums, threats, and most of the other control tactics covered in this chapter. But the beauty of it is, they don't really have to *do* any of these things very often. They simply act as if they *will* get you (or cause you to be gotten) if you step out of line. The fourth-grade bully doesn't have to take Herbie aside and say, "You little creep, if you tell the teacher I took your lunch money I'll kill you!" All he has to do is give Herbie his Tough Guy look a few times during geography class, and maybe clench his fist. Herbie's active imagination will do the rest.

Intimidators require three things in order to work their particular form of magic. First, they need a reputation. Some real

30

power helps in this regard (position as school principal, a large, fierce physical appearance, a personal relationship with the boss, a red Ferrari Testaverde), but they also must establish that they are willing to use their power to crush you like a bug with no thought for their own safety or the slightest feeling of remorse. Second, they need a set of intimidating moves: ways to let you know you'd better watch it. Skilled intimidators have honed this part of it to an art form. They can reduce their target to neurotic jelly from across a large room without even interrupting their conversation. And third, every now and then intimidators need to be willing actually to crush someone like a bug. But this is simply to keep their reputations well polished; it doesn't have much to do with control *per se,* and usually doesn't have to be done very often.

Possibly the most famous intimidation anecdote in the popular literature is found in Mario Puzo's *The Godfather.* A Hollywood producer refuses a request that a certain actor be given a part in a certain film. One morning, the producer wakes to find the severed head of his most beloved (and expensive) racehorse in his bed. It is as much the cold insanity of the act (and the obvious fact that the Godfather's men could get past the producer's guards and other security measures with such ease) as the implied threat to the producer's life that persuades him that further resistance is useless. He grants the Godfather's request.

31

Less dramatic examples of intimidation abound in everyday life. It could be that a writing assignment you wanted and are sure you deserved was given to another, less experienced co-worker. After careful consideration, you decide to convey your dissatisfaction to your boss. The co-worker in question gets wind of your plan and "just happens" to stop by your office. He proceeds to tell you about the terrific time he had over the weekend —sailing and playing tennis with the boss. "I'll never win away an assignment from someone who's connected like that," you think—and you don't try.

The PTA meeting seems as if it will never end and most of the people attending are either fidgeting in their seats or have glazed looks in their eyes. For the past half hour they have rubber-stamped every idea put before them, but now a topic that matters to you has come up for discussion and you disagree with the PTA president's position on it. You want to say so, but just as you are about to open your mouth to speak you hear coughing— the sort of dry, forced coughing someone might use to get a salesclerk's attention. You glance in the direction of that sound and spot a neighbor whose reputation as a troublemaking gossip has always made you wary of her. She glares at you menacingly. You sink back in your seat and say nothing.

Reason and Logic

Some individuals are so rational and logical they seem to function almost like computers. (To my knowledge, the first person to refer to super-rational people as operating in "computer mode" was the brilliant author and family therapist Virginia Satir.) They don't usually have much respect for feelings and intuition, or for people who allow such things to muddy up their decision-making process. To them, reason is king. If you can't give super-rational people as many reasons for going to Vermont this Christmas as they can give you for going to Hawaii, why then you must not want your vacation choice as badly as they want theirs. Or maybe you want it as badly, but if you can't even defend your position you certainly don't deserve it as much! Anyway, get out your bathing suit, because the chances are you'll be spending Christmas on the beach.

Control freaks use logical argument the way a manic carpenter uses a hammer: when his nail hits a knot in the wood, he swings faster and harder, until either the nail is driven home or it bends and is crushed into the surface of the wood. You see, a computer-mode person *knows* that he is nearly always right, that his solutions and priorities are generally best for him, for you, and for everyone else.

If you disagree with such people, they simply conclude that they haven't explained themselves well enough to you yet. So they will dredge up five or ten more reasons why you should get a mini-van instead of a station wagon, or why you should vacation this Christmas in Hawaii rather than in Vermont. The possibility that you may simply have a difference of opinion with them or, God forbid, may have a valid point, likely will never cross their minds. They will act as if coming up with the most reasons or the best argument automatically entitles them to have their own way.

Erosion

Sometimes the most effective control tactic is simple repetition. Your opponent may not need to overpower or outthink you, but simply to outlast you. Control freaks skilled at such tactics don't necessarily have to try better, or harder. They simply have to try *again*. They keep at you until they wear you out, wear you down, or wear away your resistance. Eventually you give in because it's the only way you know how to escape, or because you can't think of any other way to get them to stop.

Remember Meredith, the department store buyer who couldn't believe she'd agreed to go out with the fast-talking salesman? In retrospect she realized, "I ran out of excuses not to. Every time he made a sales call to the store, he asked me out—for that night, the next night, the night after that. He wouldn't just take no for an answer either. He had to know why, and no matter what I told him he had some sort of comeback. It was like we were having a debate about whether or not I'd go out with him and he outlasted me." Many an erosion expert will.

Controllers often use erosion in tandem with other tactics: they sell you on their ideas, they make you feel guilty, they stare you down to intimidate you. They can be stubborn, taking a position and sticking to it come hell or high water. They may be know-it-alls who feel compelled to have the last word, or show-offs who take center stage and monopolize all conversations. Like overzealous district attorneys, they may conduct seemingly endless interrogations, asking you to explain *your* position over and over again. Others are needlers who poke at your sore spots until you explode, or naggers who keep at you until you do what they want.

Logical argument and erosion go together hand in glove: the computer-mode person doesn't just out-argue you, she wears you down as well. The points she makes may or may not be valid, but after a while your brain has gone numb and you just don't care anymore. Your back aches, your neck is stiff, you have to go to the bathroom—and you'll agree to almost anything just to get out of the room. Top negotiators know this; some of them train for major contract negotiations in much the same way professional athletes prepare for a race or an important game. They've learned on the firing line that in the final analysis, persistence and stamina are as important as knowledge and verbal skill. In smaller ways we all have experienced this as well. For instance, everyone has been worn down by "Yes, but . . ." tactics used by people who seemingly can find something wrong with any conceivable idea or plan. Remember, it's almost never the first or second rebuttal that gets you to throw in the towel, it's the twenty-fifth or thirtieth. Eventually you think, "I don't *need* this, life is too short." You're right, of course, life is too short; but it's still game, set, and match to the computer-mode eroder.

Indirect Control Tactics

There are a tremendous number of ways to exert "hidden" control, and control freaks seem to know most of them. In the real world these moves are nearly always used in combination with several other direct and indirect ploys. The resulting strategies can be incredibly complex and subtle; they can be extremely hard to recognize, and even harder to escape.

Short-Circuiting

Rick doesn't want his wife, Karen, to return a phone call from her ex-husband, so he never gives her the message. Emma wants Lisa to fly with her to visit relatives the week before the wedding, so she purchases and pays for nonrefundable airline tickets —before clearing the arrangement with Lisa. And Warren thinks it's dangerous for women to go out after dark, so he hides his wife's car keys. Each of these controllers used a short-circuiting tactic: they wanted to achieve a certain outcome, but for reasons of their own chose not to be direct with the other person about it. So, instead, they *manipulated the situation* in a way that made it difficult or impossible for the other person to do anything but go along.

Short-circuiters can play on your need for a job, the fact that you have a final exam coming up, or simply that you want to get your kids to school on time. Here the controller doesn't have to create the restrictive circumstances, but only take advantage of ones that already exist. (Of course, a real control freak would give those circumstances a couple of extra twists, and then throw in a small bribe or two on general principles.) Also, his or her job is made much easier when the other person believes that their situation permits no other choice.

For instance, Barbara continues to work for a chauvinistic boss because she is a single parent with no particular clout in the job market. She puts a high priority on feeding her children, so she puts up with her boss's disrespectful comments, sexual innuendos, and general harassment—and occasionally goes to dinner with him as well—because she feels she has to. Many women have chosen to stay in bad marriages with boorish, abusive husbands for the same reasons. When asked why they put up with such treatment, they often respond, "I know I should do something about it, but I don't know what to do. I can't leave him—I love him. Besides, where else would I go?"

WHEN SHORT-CIRCUITING BECOMES ENTRAPMENT

Technically, other alternatives do exist for people like Barbara. Spouse abuse is a crime, and there are shelters where abused women can go. Sexual harassment on the job is also illegal. Who knows, Barbara may has enough evidence to bring her boss up on charges. But Barbara's boss buys her off with more than a paycheck. He allows her to work flextime, so she can pick up her youngest from kindergarten—and when the sitter doesn't show up, lets her bring the child with her to the office. Victims of abuse and harassment should certainly take advantage of the alternatives available to them. But in the real world, it is often very difficult for such people to assume the risks and accept the sacrifices that would almost certainly be part of the package.

Short-circuiting tactics are commonly used by codependents to try to control the addicts with whom they are entangled. "I would do just about anything to keep my mother from drinking!", said Warren during a meeting for adult children of alcoholics. "As a ten-year-old child, I would watch as she brought in the groceries after work. If she went into the bathroom before putting them away, I knew she was hiding a bottle, and as soon as I could do so without arousing her suspicion I would go in myself to look for it.

"I learned early very quickly that simply stealing Mother's bottle or pouring it out didn't work—I'd get beaten and sent to my room, and she would just get a new bottle. But I found that if I was careful about it, I could pour out about half the contents and replace it with water. If Mother'd already had a couple of drinks she generally wouldn't notice. I know this doesn't sound like much of a solution, but at least she wouldn't get drunk so quickly. And at the time, I really thought I was helping us both.''

Now it's twenty years later, and of course Warren doesn't live with his mother anymore. Instead, he is married to a woman who has a serious eating disorder; and even Warren can see similarities between the ways he tries to ''help'' his wife and the strategies that allowed him to cope with an alcoholic parent when he was ten years old.

Deception

36

This is the ''lie, cheat, and steal'' category. Controllers misrepresent reality, concealing or disguising anything they think might prevent you from buying what they are selling. Deception works for the most obvious of reasons: you take the controllers at their word, and act accordingly. What's more, since skilled deceivers will tell you what you want to hear in the first place, you resent being controlled in this manner only when you discover the deception.

Deception tactics run the gamut from outright lies to subtle implications and omissions intended to leave you with a false impression. The controller may promise to do one thing and then do another—falsify information about herself in order land a job, or simply order a dinner in an elegant restaurant and then leave without paying for it. Seduction tactics usually fall into this category, as does most flattery. ''Carrot-dangling''—a form of bribery in which the payoff appears to be available throughout the transaction, but then is withdrawn at the last minute—falls here as well.

A business associate may play ''bandwagon,'' telling you that everyone else has already agreed to their plan—that is, jumped on the bandwagon—or that people are saying you're difficult to deal with (and this is your chance to prove that you're not). An acquaintance may play the part of your best buddy, assuring you over and over again that he or she is on your side and looking out for your interests—and then proceed to rob you blind.

In addition, there are subtler forms of deception which are

intended to work over a period of time. Gradually, stitch by stitch, the deceiver weaves a tapestry of little lies and half-truths that can come to be more powerful and more destructive than almost any other form of control. Taken out of context, any one of the individual tactics would seem trivial, certainly too small to make a fuss over. But five years later you're a basket case. This pattern is sometimes called "gaslighting," after the classic motion picture in which a host of little lies were used to try to drive a woman crazy.

One common gaslighting tactic involves playing *just a little* dumb. In the following scene, a husband and wife are sitting in the living room after dinner. There is a *TV Guide* on the coffee table immediately in front of the husband.

WIFE: What's on TV tonight, honey?

HUSBAND: I don't know.

WIFE: Uh, isn't that the *Guide* on the table there in front of you?

HUSBAND: Uh-huh.

WIFE: Well?

HUSBAND: Well, what?

The husband acts as if he doesn't understand, or didn't hear, what his wife said. She is kept in a slightly one-down position, constantly having to explain or repeat herself. Over time, this can have an absolutely mind-boggling effect; its victim gradually begins to think it may really be her fault, may come to doubt her own experience and the judgments she bases on that experience.

Deception is generally used in combination with other ploys. For instance, the husband might answer his wife's annoyed response with a kind of "psychological imperialism," interpreting her actions in a way that undermines her power or makes her look like the culprit:

WIFE: *(Angrily)* God, John, I hate it when you do this. Why can't you just look in the *Guide?*

HUSBAND: *(Looking at his wife as if she's nuts)* Gee, you're touchy tonight. Must be that time of the month again.

37

When confronted, deceptive controllers will try to excuse their behavior in one way or another. They may claim they made an honest mistake, that you misheard them, or that the whole thing was a misunderstanding. If you buy that innocent act, you have been deceived again.

Emotional Exploitation

When someone controls or manipulates you *by taking advantage of the fact that you care for them,* you have been emotionally exploited. Of course, in little ways we all do exactly that from time to time—it's human nature. Teresa goes on a bit about the pulled muscle she got playing Ultimate Frisbee so that Dudley will give her a back rub. When Roger comes home from college for the holidays he never lifts a finger around the house; he knows his mother misses him a great deal and won't mind picking up after him for a week or so. But hopefully most of us give as good as we get, and in the long run the ledger comes within a ballpark or two of breaking even.

In Chapter 1 it was mentioned that there is nothing necessarily wrong with control, and that, depending on the circumstances, even control freaks can sometimes be handy to have around. The same can be said for most control tactics. Logic, short-circuiting, deception, takeover, even intimidation and attack can be useful tools and sometimes are used to help rather than hurt. This is *not* true of exploitation tactics. *At best,* the innocent, "human nature" exploitation moves mentioned earlier don't cause much harm. But when emotional exploitation is taken to the extreme, it can cause more pain than any of the other methods—pain which can literally go on at maximum intensity for years.

But exploitation is also incredibly powerful; and anything so powerful will be used, and used often. A great many of us, controllers and accommodators alike, use these methods to excess. Many popular books have been written on the subject; the benchmark *play* in this area would, of course, be *Who's Afraid of Virginia Woolf?* by Edward Albee. But you don't have to delve into literature to get a sense of how these patterns operate—just turn on the TV any weekday afternoon. Emotional exploitation is the meat-and-potatoes device of all television soap operas.

In emotional exploitation, the control freak supplies the specific tactic, and you supply the love or caring which empowers it. The verbal statements a controller makes are sometimes called *emotional hooks,* because they "hook" your feelings and make you vulnerable to manipulation. Exploitation tactics include implications, double messages, either/or thinking and forced-choice maneuvers ("Either you go to bed with me tonight or I'll know you don't love me."), accusations, sarcasm, anger, tears, guilt and a host of other verbal and emotional ploys. The list is mix-and-match; skilled exploiters tend to use a kind of shotgun approach, throwing everything at you but the kitchen sink.

The following examples contain just a few of their most common maneuvers. How many of them can you recognize?

Inducing Guilt George had just settled down in front of the television when the phone rang. His son was on the line. When he immediately apologized for bothering him, George knew what was coming and vowed not to move from his spot on the sofa, no matter what. But then his son said, "Dad I'm desperate. Both of my cooks are out sick. My dishwasher didn't show up. If you don't come down here to help out, I'm going to have to shut the doors. I mean it, actually close the place on a Saturday night for the first time in twenty years. With all the competition around here, you know that'll be the kiss of death for the business."

George started to feel that horrible twinge in his belly, and then his son threw in the clincher: "If you really cared about what happens to me, you would understand how much I need your help. And how hard it is for me when you make me beg." George's resolution not to drop everything to bail out his son fell apart in the face of George Jr.'s guilt tactics. Rationally, he was pretty sure the restaurant could survive without him, and he certainly wanted to see the end of that basketball game. Furthermore, at some level he knew exactly what his son was doing. But, well . . . maybe he, George, *had* been a little selfish lately, maybe he could help just this once. . . . George shrugged helplessly, turned off the TV, and headed for the door.

Most of us learned to feel guilty early and well; those buttons are still in there waiting to be pushed by anyone who knows how. And knowing how is a specialty of control freaks.

Pouting Pouting is a double message pattern you've undoubtedly come across. Generally the pouter's words say one thing (or, if he is silent, they say nothing), while his nonverbal

39

behavior and tone of voice make a very clear and very different statement. Often implications, veiled accusations, disconnection, and various other tactics are used as well.

Karen has dinner with her husband Rick, helps to wash the dishes and then says, "Well, I'm off to my women's group meeting. See you around nine, honey." The following conversation ensues:

RICK: *(Sighs)*

KAREN: "What's wrong, Rick?"

RICK: *(Bleakly)* "Oh, nothing . . ."

KAREN: "Rick, I *hate* this. If you don't want me to go out tonight, why don't you just say so?"

RICK: *(As the long-suffering martyr)* "No, no, you can go, that's okay. Far be it from me to keep you from your precious meeting. I'll be okay, don't worry . . . I've got the TV set and the dog to play with. . . ."

40

Karen, of course, knows there's something wrong. She and Rick go a couple of more rounds, she getting progressively angrier, he more long-suffering. Eventually Karen yells something she'll feel guilty about later, and slams out the door. She spends her time at the women's group alternately feeling enraged at the way Rick treated her and nervous about what will happen at home later that night.

Or maybe Rick succeeds in getting his wife to stay home. Annoyed at her husband for the obvious manipulation and at herself for having given into it, Karen does not have a pleasant evening. That night, she and Rick sleep on opposite sides of the bed. The next morning, Rick wakes up in a great mood; but Karen is still angry. At breakfast she is finally able to confront her husband about the pouting behavior he used to keep her from her women's group meeting.

Rick, of course, responds with surprise and indignation. "Don't look at me, Karen," he says as if butter wouldn't melt in his mouth. "I didn't keep you from going to your meeting. Hell, *I* told you to go." And so he did.

Scorekeeping   One variation on this tactic involves invoking past favors, sometimes over and over again. It works best when most of the important communication is nonverbal.

Two old friends are having a drink together. Fred says, "Hey, Al, I need a ride to the airport at about seven-thirty Friday morning. Could you take me?" Al, who is tired of his friend's seemingly constant requests, says, "Gee, my granddaughter is in town this week. I was planning to spend the morning with her." Fred sits quietly for a minute or so, staring into his beer, and then says with *just a touch* of sadness, "I'm a little surprised, old buddy. I mean, after I saved your life on the beach at Anzio during the Big One . . . I guess you've forgotten. . . ." Now, Fred did save Al's life during World War II. But that was thirty-six years ago. And Al certainly hasn't forgotten, because since then Fred has brought it up at least five hundred times when asking Al for a favor or a small loan.

Emotional exploitation works in part because you begin to doubt yourself. When the right button is pushed, a little voice comes on in your head, saying, "Gee, maybe he's right—maybe I *am* being selfish. It wouldn't hurt to help him out just this once." At this point the odds have changed: now it's you and him against you. You're outnumbered, and down to the restaurant or off to the airport you go.

41

Disconnection

Disconnectors control you by totally or partially withdrawing from you. Their power comes from the fact that you need (or think you need) to interact with them in some way. So they don't return your phone calls. They change the subject, or walk away in the middle of conversations. They withhold sex, turn up the stereo while you are talking to them, lock themselves in the bathroom, or simply give you the silent treatment. Or they stonewall you when you need their cooperation to work out a problem, resolve a conflict, or get a project completed. This last variation is particularly popular among employees who for one reason or another (civil service, union contracts, tenure, value to company, nepotism) either can't be fired or don't care.

Pouting and other emotional exploitation ploys often have a disconnection component. Here are a couple of additional variations on the theme.

Triangulation   You're being *triangulated* when the control freak uses a third party to manipulate or disempower you. One common variation cuts you out of the communication loop in one way or another. For instance, an employee takes a complaint directly to the company president rather than first trying to work things out with her supervisor. Or, Martha criticizes Jane to Mary, knowing that Mary will leak the criticism back to Jane.

Another variation, called *third-party referencing,* involves controllers cutting themselves out of the loop. Debbie tells her mother she's decided to postpone college for a year to get some practical work experience. Mom, who doesn't like that idea at all, says in a worried tone of voice, "Well, honey, whatever you think is best is all right by me. But your father is going to be *crushed. . . ."*

Intimidation   The threat of disconnection is a very powerful intimidation tool. As with other intimidation tactics, control freaks don't really have to do anything—they simply need to give the impression they *will* withdraw or leave if their unfortunate partner doesn't mind his or her P's and Q's. For a great many people, the fear of being rejected and left alone absolutely overrides all else, and they literally will go to any lengths to avoid that most terrifying of eventualities. Even little disconnections are difficult for such people. They believe being left permanently would be devastating, something they simply could not face. And so, when the control freak threatens to leave, or when he or she begins to play "one foot out the door," they cave in, and become putty in his hands.

Entrapment

Simple traps work in much the same way as exploitation. That is, the controller hooks you by using your emotional reactions against you. But exploiters play on your feelings for *them;* entrapment ploys can utilize any strong feeling. Fear, confusion, grief, and hope are common examples. (The complex control traps which we'll get to in Chapter 3 are much broader in scope. Among other things, they aren't set up by the control freak—the control freak is just as trapped in them as the accommodator is.) Basically, you find yourself boxed into a no-win situation. Whatever you do, you're wrong—and you have to do something; you can't choose not to act. One of the simplest ways controllers create this kind of setup is to ask a question they *already know the answer to,* in order to embarrass you, prove you wrong, punish you or put you on the spot. If you are unfortunate enough to answer incorrectly, whammo!

The Trap Question Kim, a twenty-eight-year-old teacher's aide, got trapped when her boyfriend, Alan, asked her where she wanted to go for her birthday dinner. Since she was accustomed to having Alan plan their activities and because where they ate really did not matter to her, Kim told Alan that he could decide.

"I hate it when you do that," Alan snapped. "I'm asking you to tell me what you think. I mean, you do think, don't you?"

Stung but not showing it, Kim complied with Alan's demand. She told him what she thought, mentioning a half-dozen restaurants she liked. He vetoed every suggestion, making snide comments about each option she offered. Kim said, "After he made sure I felt like I had no taste, no class, and not a brain in my head, we ended up at his favorite restaurant, which was probably where he wanted us to go all along."

What did Alan get from this interaction? In addition to dinner at the restaurant of his choice, he got to feel superior and in control. That is a major payoff for anyone who uses entrapment.

Double Binds Double messages were mentioned earlier in connection with emotional exploitation. However, when the double message is accompanied by an implied demand *to ignore the contradiction involved,* something much worse can develop.

Peter and Mary have serious marital problems. Among other things, Peter drinks, and when he drinks he sometimes becomes violent. So far, his treatment of Mary in this regard hasn't progressed past an occasional slap. But for Mary, that's enough (as it should be)! The slaps sting, Mary knows her husband has a terrible temper, and recently his drinking's been getting worse. Mary is frightened.

She loves her husband, and would like to talk things out with him. But when not angry, Peter just laughs and tells her she's exaggerating. If she brings the subject up when he is angry, he loudly (and angrily) denies (1) that he has ever slapped her, and (2) that he is angry now.

Mary feels as if she's slowly going mad. At this point, she is afraid that if she says something like, "Gee, honey, you say you're not angry, but you sure sound angry," Peter might become even more enraged, and physically harm her. Her other

43

alternative is to act as if she's not aware of Peter's anger—but she feels far too frightened and lonely to do that. She is really stuck.

If things get bad enough, Mary's mind may solve the problem for her by altering reality (or Mary's experience of reality) just enough so Mary can live there in relative peace. Eventually Mary may get to the point where she *literally is no longer aware* her husband is sending very aggressive, contradictory messages. She isn't just ignoring them; as far as her conscious mind is concerned, the anger signals aren't there anymore. Of course, Mary's stomach hurts, and she often feels nervous without knowing why. And she is no longer quite so able to avoid getting slapped.

Being forced to deny one's own experience in order to survive is one of the most deadly and destructive of control traps. It is one example of a set of incredibly powerful patterns psychologists call *double binds.* At their worst, double binds don't just perplex you, they immobilize you. You are incapable of moving in any direction because the ambiguity and incongruencies in the messages you are receiving put you in a paralyzing "damned if you do, damned if you don't, *and damned if you don't play"* position. Then the control freak can move in at his leisure and take over, making demands which you, in your befuddled and entrapped state, find impossible to refuse.

Final Thoughts

Control freaks often use the methods described in this chapter, and use them to the extreme. Furthermore, they often can't *stop* using them, even when the tactics clearly are no longer working. For many control freaks, controlling becomes more important than reaching whatever goal may have induced them to take over in the first place. They will fight desperately to stay in the driver's seat, using any and all methods they think will help. As you begin to look for and recognize these (and other) control tactics, here are some final thoughts to keep in mind.

1. Control tactics are almost never used one at a time (as we describe them here). Major-league controllers know they don't have to choose between options—they can use them all. They size you up, they set you up and then they move in. And, depending on the circumstances, the

best of them can do it without your even being aware what's happening. By the time you've recognized tactic number 1, they're already throwing tactics 7, 9, and 13B at you.

2. Different individuals tend to use different tactic patterns. Learn to recognize and anticipate these patterns. On the other hand, don't rely on your control freak's using a particular pattern in a particular situation just because he or she has done so in the past. Skilled controllers will vary their strategies, particularly when they realize you are beginning to catch on to them.

3. Some tactics are used outright to control people. But others are called into play only when control freaks sense (rightly or wrongly) that they may be losing control. These are crisis tactics, measures intended to get things back in line. Of course, some individuals are always in crisis mode. But most controllers don't use these tactics all, or even much of the time. When they are in control and things are going smoothly, they may act in a reasonable and flexible manner. The methods they use to influence the people and situations around them may be gentle, respectful, even benign. But when something begins to go wrong, watch out.

Follow-up: Examining Your Achilles' Heel

Which control tactics are most likely to get to you? Select one general tactic (such as assault, deception, erosion) or specific move (such as ridicule, double messages, trap questions) and think about a time in the recent past when someone used it on you. Then, in a notebook or on a sheet of paper, write your answers to the following questions.

1. Who used the move or tactic on you? What sort of relationship do you have with that person and how important to you is that relationship?

2. What was going on when the move was made? What happened before, during and after it? A general descrip-

tion will suffice. However, you can gain more useful insights by re-creating the entire interaction as if it were a scene from a movie you were watching. Describe both words and actions and jot down any pertinent background information.

3. Although you may not have been consciously aware of them at the time, see if you can remember any thoughts that might have run through your mind (such as "Uh-oh. I just said something he didn't like"; "If I don't say I agree with her, she'll go on about this all night"), and any feelings that might have washed over you (anger, fear, rejection).

4. What was the outcome of the interaction? (Did the controller get his or her way? Did you do or say something you immediately or later regretted? Were you distracted from or prevented from pursuing your goals?)

5. How typical was that outcome? (Is what happened what usually happens when that person or someone else in your life makes that particular control move?)

Your answers to these questions provide the first threads for understanding how control tactics can be used against you. Hang on to your answer sheets. Later on in the book we'll teach you the most effective ways to deal with controllers and their methods. But for now, be content with learning to recognize them. As you will see, being able to identify control patterns *before* they ensnare you is really half the battle.

In the next chapter, we'll take a look at the other side of the coin: the tactics and styles accommodators typically use when responding to a control freak.

3

I'M YOURS

How We Accommodate the Control Freaks in Our Lives

No question about it, control freaks are difficult people to deal with. They have a tremendous array of tactics at their disposal and have been practicing combinations of these tactics since before they learned to talk. They have the need to control you, the intent to control you, and often are willing to sacrifice a great deal, including the very outcomes they hope to achieve, simply to *succeed* in controlling you. But *they still can't do it alone—* they need your help. And that's where accommodation comes in.

In the last chapter, we met Kim and Alan as they were getting ready to go out to celebrate Kim's birthday. As you may recall, Alan, who usually planned every aspect of the couple's dates, unexpectedly asked Kim where she wanted to dine. Kim obligingly made some suggestions; but after a few rounds of "Why don't we . . . ?" "Yes, but . . ." they wound up at a restaurant of Alan's choosing.

At the restaurant, Alan, who knew a great deal about fine wines and had been sharing his knowledge with Kim since their first meeting, selected an expensive bottle and when it arrived, administered a pop quiz—asking Kim various questions to determine how much she had learned. Kim obediently submitted to and passed the test, breathing a sigh of relief. (Had she missed a question, she would have been forced to hear the entire wine lecture once more.)

When it came time to order from the rather extensive menu, Alan told Kim what he thought she would like. Irritated, Kim ordered something else. "You're going to be disappointed," Alan warned her. She was, but not wanting to hear Alan's "I told you so," she assured him that her meal was delicious and devoured every tasteless morsel of it.

After dinner, Alan and Kim went to a movie that Alan's favorite critic had proclaimed a masterpiece, and Alan had felt sure Kim would enjoy. She was not particularly impressed with it, although Alan was. "What a great, great movie," he declared as they left the theater. Kim said nothing. "Didn't you think it was terrific?" he asked. Like most people who use "Didn't you . . ." questions, Alan was interested less in Kim's reaction than in her blanket endorsement of his opinion. But she missed her cue.

"It was okay," Kim replied unenthusiastically.

"What?" Alan barked, stopping dead in his tracks. "You didn't like it?!" He could not have been more indignant if he had written, produced and directed the movie himself. "How could you *not* like it?" he gasped and proceeded to expound on the film's virtues.

Ten minutes later, when she could finally get a word in edgewise, Kim reversed herself. Yes, it had been a great movie, she assured him, and yes, now that she had given it more thought, she did love it.

"He didn't actually change my opinion," Kim explained. "I just knew he wouldn't let up on me until I agreed with him, and so I did." Alan was assuaged and in a matter of moments was acting as if nothing had happened. But Kim's evening was ruined. She spent the next few hours nervously watching her step and carefully choosing her words in hopes of getting through the rest of their night out without another incident. Between her anxiety and the blaring disco music at the nightclub Alan insisted they go to, she wound up with a monster headache.

Accommodation

If Kim and Alan's night out was scored like a college wrestling match, with points awarded for takedowns, reversals, and riding time, it certainly wouldn't be difficult to pick a winner. Throughout the evening, Alan systematically went after what he wanted and got it while Kim almost exclusively *reacted* to what Alan did or said. Alan controlled Kim with setups and putdowns, and with an array of trapping maneuvers that left

Kim dizzy. Confused and uncertain, she went right along with him.

Whether she was passing up the opportunity to make a decision or ignoring an uncalled-for remark, saying what she thought Alan wanted to hear or obediently submitting to his surprise quizzes, taking a symbolic stand on what to order for dinner, concealing her disappointment with her meal, or pretending to agree with Alan's movie review, Kim's words and actions were dictated by Alan's. And since Alan got exactly what he wanted and was able to feel superior and in control, Kim's responses obviously worked to his advantage and did absolutely nothing to discourage him from using the same or similar tactics on her again.

Of course, you may be thinking that if you were in Kim's shoes, you wouldn't have let Alan get away with his cutting remarks and condescending comments. *You* would have told him precisely where to put his bottle of wine and know-it-all attitude. And you certainly would have defended your right to not like a movie no matter how much artistic merit Alan said it had. You might have had a half dozen arguments with Alan, but at least he wouldn't have controlled you.

Don't be too sure about that.

Fighting back against control tactics may look and feel different from giving in to them. And if you had to choose between those and only those alternatives, fighting back might most often be the better choice. But in the long run, giving in and fighting back are little more than different sides of the same coin. After all, would spending an entire evening resisting and arguing with Alan *really* leave you any better off than Kim was? Probably not, unless you just happen to like fighting with control freaks. Alan isn't going to change. Over time, whether you give in to the controller in your life or fight back against him, it's almost guaranteed you won't be pleased with the results. In the long run, both are losing propositions.

That said, let's take a look at six of the most common giving-in and fighting-back accommodation styles.

Giving In

When faced with real or potential conflict, many of us tend to give in, changing ourselves to conform with the controller's

49

needs and wishes. This is not to say we *always* yield; under certain circumstances, or when pushed over the edge, we may fight like wildcats. But our natural tendency is to acquiesce. Motivated by fear, guilt, a sense of obligation, or a desire to avoid conflict, we allow controllers to get their own way with no resistance and even some assistance—permitting them to think that they have influenced our thoughts, feelings and actions or that their words and actions didn't bother us.

Peacekeeping

Kim was a peacekeeper. She saw no point in actively resisting Alan's control. Doing so would have led to an argument she stood no chance of winning. Getting angry at Alan for trying to control her was also out of the question. Anger was an emotion that disturbed Kim and which she rarely allowed herself to feel, much less express. Her motivation for giving in (or appearing to give in) was to avoid hassles, uproars, attacks or angry tirades.

Is There a Peacekeeper in You?   If you have little tolerance for anger and dissent, feel uncomfortable simply witnessing an argument, and anxious or threatened when other people disagree with you, then control freaks may bring out the peacekeeper in you too.

As a peacekeeper, *"Don't rock the boat!"* is your motto. Avoiding conflicts at all costs is your goal. You would like to get along with everyone. You wish that other people would try harder to get along with each other, and at a fundamental level you believe that even minor conflicts can lead to full-scale battles that could ultimately destroy you or your relationship.

In general, you watch your step, considering other people's probable reactions before taking actions on your own. You censor yourself, saying whatever will be least likely to upset people or start arguments instead of what you really think or mean. And you assign yourself the role of identifying common ground, rushing in to find points of agreement that might end a conflict —but not necessarily resolve it.

If asked, you will say that arguments are more trouble than they're worth and that you'd rather let things go than waste time and energy bickering about them. But deep down inside you are afraid that if people who matter to you get angry, they might go away and never come back. Consequently, the closer you are to someone, the harder you try to keep the peace, some-times to the point of weighing and measuring every word you utter and every move you make.

If you are prone to peacekeeping, the control tactics that are most likely to get to you are assaults, coercion and intimidation, or anything that may lead you to believe that arguments or criti-cism could be forthcoming. In addition to those Kim used, typi-cal peacekeeping responses include:

- backing down at the first sign of disagreement.
- flattering and second-guessing people to prevent them from getting angry.
- placating, appeasing and pacifying people when they do express anger or dissatisfaction.
- conniving or sneaking around in order to get your more pressing needs met (for example, getting your own way by convincing control freaks that something you want is their idea or doing what you want but making sure con-trol freaks don't find out about it).

People Pleasing

Beverly described the day Ellen gave her a gift to show how much she valued their friendship and simultaneously criticized her for not acting like a good friend the night before. Shaking her head in dismay, Beverly tried to explain why that double message had such a powerful impact on her. "Sure, it was a pretty sneaky way to stick it to me," Beverly said. "But what really hurts is that I try so hard to be nice to Ellen. Whenever I go anywhere, I invite her to go with me. I call or visit her every day, just to touch base and let her know I care. I even send over dinner for her and her husband when I'm cooking something I know they like. And at that church social, I went out of my way to make sure she was comfortable and having a good time. For Pete's sake, what more does that woman want from me?"

Whatever that might be, it was clear that Beverly would con-tinue to go out of her way to give it to Ellen. Beverly tended to *people-please.* She snapped to attention and followed Ellen's or-ders, rearranged her schedule to better suit Ellen's meticulous plans, changed her clothes if Ellen criticized them, and bent over backward to show Ellen she cared. She believed that being good

51

to people and doing whatever she could to make them happy was the best way to be accepted by them and to feel good about herself.

Are You a People-Pleaser?   If you care a great deal that people view you as kind, giving, responsible or indispensable, are sensitive to criticism or hate to be ignored, and devote a great deal of your time and energy to making other people happy, boosting their egos or seeking their praise and approval, then control freaks may bring out the people-pleaser in you too. Because you tend to be highly motivated to maintain the warmth and closeness in your relationships and look to others to validate your worth, you are especially vulnerable to disconnecting control moves as well as emotional exploitation, intimidation, bribes, warnings and, of course, criticism. Deceptive tactics, most notably those involving flattery, also get to you quite easily. You tend to:

- quickly correct anything controllers criticize.
- check with controllers to make sure they approve of your plans.
- make up for displeasing people by giving them their way and then some. (For instance, if you ''made'' your daughter unhappy when you couldn't drive her to the mall on Tuesday, you not only give her a ride on Wednesday, but also offer her extra spending money.)
- ''chase'' people who sulk, pout or otherwise withdraw from you, pampering, coaxing and trying to draw them out of their shells or trying to guess what is bothering them and then doing whatever you can to make them feel better.

Self-Sacrifice

Remember Sam, the free-lance photographer who was intimidated by Cassie, one of his employers? His immediate response to Cassie's attack was to apologize for provoking it—even though he had not actually done anything to warrant such a vicious tirade. He instantaneously shelved his doubts and accepted Cassie's assignment without asking for the assurances he needed and deserved. And when the problems Sam predicted did indeed arise, he handled them himself—even though they were not his responsibility and consumed time and energy he could have used more productively.

"I know I should have told Cassie what was going on," Sam acknowledged. "I definitely could have used her support. But she seemed so stressed out and overwhelmed already that I just couldn't bring myself to do it." And so Sam shouldered the burden alone, becoming stressed out and overwhelmed himself. Cassie initially overpowered him, bullying and scaring Sam into taking that burden off her hands. But Sam drove himself the extra mile. He was a *self-sacrificer*—he gave up his goals to help other people reach theirs and allowed his needs to go unmet so that other people would be able to fulfill theirs.

Are You a Self-Sacrificer? If you tend to believe that other people's wishes and needs are more important than your own, if you are prone to make sacrifices for the "greater good" of your relationships, family or company, and are apt to blame yourself or wonder what you did wrong whenever things aren't running smoothly, then the self-sacrificer in you may be making life easier for control freaks too.

Like peacekeepers, you are allergic to anger. Like people-pleasers you want other people to be happy and comfortable. Indeed, you hate to see them suffer, so much so that you are willing to suffer yourself just to make sure that they don't. No matter how much is heaped upon you, you believe you can take it. To prove it you regularly and repeatedly give in to control freaks' demands while rarely if ever making demands of your own. Sometimes you actually decide what other people need and give it to them *before* they ask.

Because you feel guilty even when you haven't done anything wrong, you are particularly susceptible to emotionally exploitative control tactics and mind-boggling double messages—especially the "It's okay" (deep sigh), "don't worry about me" variety. The eroder's repetitive, persuasive arguments and the intimidator's implication that something horrible will happen if you fail to come through also trigger automatic, habitual self-sacrificing responses, such as:

- saying yes to any request for assistance—no matter how busy you are.

- giving in to people who suggest you could hurt or offend them in any way.

- making amends to people who imply that you have already hurt or offended them in some way.

- working around or picking up the slack for people who play dumb or act helpless.

- justifying their behavior to others and telling yourself that it doesn't bother you, that it was caused by you, or that it is actually their way of showing they care about you.

Fighting Back

Some of us would never dream of using peacekeeping, people-pleasing or self-sacrificing behaviors. We would rather fight than switch. As soon we detect controlling behavior, especially from someone who has a history of manipulating us or pushing us around, we resist. We try to thwart the controllers in our lives—prevent them from taking advantage of us or punish them for using control tactics on us. Our own control tendencies begin to come to the surface as we begin trying to get them to stop what they are doing and see things from our point of view.

Passive Resistance

"I wish I could tell Irene to get off my case," Kelly said with a sigh; then she described one of her favorite fantasies. "Irene would show up for one of her little chats, that sickeningly sweet smile on her face, coffee mug in hand, the whole bit. But instead of just sitting there waiting for her to do her thing, I'd get up and walk toward her, stop right in front of her, point to the chair in front of my desk, and say, 'Just sit down and keep your mouth shut.' Then I'd slam the door, wheel around, and get straight to the point.

"I'd look her right in the eye and say, 'Stop treating me like an idiot. Stop looking over my shoulder and asking me stupid questions that you know the answers to in the first place. Just give it up already and let me do my job.' "

Sighing again as her vision of reading Irene the riot act faded, Kelly said, "But of course I can't do that. I can't do anything.

She's my boss. I need my job. Except for her meddling, I really *like* my job and I don't want to lose it, so my hands are tied."

But were they? Although Kelly complained there was nothing she could do to counter Irene's controlling behavior, in fact she did plenty. She just did it under the table, and in a manner that did neither woman any good.

When Irene arrived for a chat, Kelly gave her a withering look. Then, instead of returning Irene's cheery "Good morning," she immediately broke eye contact and tried to look as if she was intently concentrating on the paperwork in front of her. When Irene asked if she could come in, Kelly shrugged noncommittally. She responded to Irene's casual comments with short, sharp sentences delivered in a flat, unenthusiastic tone of voice and throughout their conversation, repeatedly checked her watch, fidgeted, yawned, or tapped her pencil against her desk. Then, when Irene finally got to the point and asked about one of Kelly's projects, she replied sarcastically, mimicking the "sickeningly sweet" tone of voice she attributed to Irene.

Relying on many of the same undermining maneuvers that control freaks use, Kelly was *passively resisting* Irene's control. Although she never came right out and said what was on her mind, everything she did (or didn't do) conveyed the message: "I have to do what you say and put up with what you do, but I don't have to like it. And I think I can make it a tad less pleasant for you as well!"

Naturally, Kelly hoped Irene would get the underlying message and back off. But, of course, Irene did just the reverse. Interpreting Kelly's resistance as an attitude problem, she became even more determined to keep an eye on her. And, as a manager who subscribed with a vengeance to that bit of folk wisdom about catching more flies with honey than with vinegar, Irene vowed to be even sweeter to Kelly next time around.

The Passive Resister in You You too may lack the power or courage to directly oppose the controlling people in your life. Speaking your mind, conveying your displeasure or refusing to go along with their plans seems like too great a risk. You might lose your job, alienate your spouse, parents or friends, make your children hate you, or gain an unwanted reputation as a troublemaker. Yet, unlike peacekeepers, people-pleasers or self-sacrificers, you cannot, or will not, suppress your feelings entirely, and you prefer not to give in to people who bully or

55

manipulate you. The passive resister inside you whispers, "You can't let them get away with this. You have to do something to stop them—*just don't get caught.*" And so you trot out a trunkful of ploys that create confusion, stir up unsettling emotions, and generally make life a little more difficult and a little less pleasant for people who try to control you. You may:

- appear testy, sullen or sarcastic (and hope that will keep controllers at arm's length or convince them to go looking for a more docile victim).

- dawdle, delay or procrastinate (and hope controllers will forget about the demands they made or get tired of waiting and handle things themselves).

- act helpless, play dumb, or ask dozens of questions "just to make sure" you understand exactly what controllers want (and hope they become so exasperated that they take care of the task themselves or go off to hassle someone else).

- tune out—stare blankly, fuss, fidget, hum—while controllers talk to or yell at you (and hope they will shut up or get fed up and go away).

In case this hasn't been made clear, passive resistance rarely gets anyone off your back. In fact, as it did in Kelly's case, your maneuvering can backfire, escalating conflicts and frustrating or infuriating control freaks who then try even harder to control you.

Retaliation

As you read about Beverly's reactions to her friend Ellen's controlling behavior page (51), you may have wondered if other people in Ellen's life responded to her in the same way. Her youngest daughter did, snapping to attention and jumping through hoops even more frantically than Beverly. Ellen's oldest stayed out of her mother's way as much as possible and moved into an apartment of her own at age eighteen. Today, she lives in Japan and speaks to her mother no more than twice a year. And Ellen's husband, Howard—how did he put up with her controlling behavior for nearly thirty years? By getting even. Unable to make Ellen stop trying to control him, he made her pay for the privilege.

After a day of listening to Ellen harp at him about everything from leaving the bathroom door open when he showered so he wouldn't steam up the mirrors to how many cocktails he could have with dinner, it was not unusual to find Howard spending the night on the sofa bed in his study. "I did what you wanted all day, but I'm sleeping where I want tonight," he would say, shutting the door behind him and locking it. In a similar move, he would declare, "I may have to listen to you, but I don't have to talk to you," and give Ellen the silent treatment. Another effective retaliation tactic, which worked particularly well at dinner parties, was to refuse to support or agree with a point his wife badly wanted to make (whether he *really* agreed with it or not). "Howard, don't you agree that's what they should do?" Ellen would ask. "No, dear," Howard would reply levelly, "I don't."

In addition to these deliberate paybacks, Howard got to Ellen in less direct ways combining retaliation with passive resistance. When Ellen sent him into the kitchen for the fourth time in fifteen minutes, he did not *intentionally* knock the cocktail sauce off the coffee table onto the spotless white rug. It just happened, like so many other "accidents" that seemed to happen when he and Ellen were together. When he scheduled evening or weekend business meetings and swore that Ellen had not told him about other engagements, he was not lying. He frequently forgot about the plans Ellen made for the two of them. He did not spend an hour in the bathroom just so Ellen would go into a panic about being late. It really took him that long to get ready to go out for the evening. Over the years he had gotten slower and slower. And he made more and more mistakes. "I'm only human," he would say quite sincerely when he took a wrong turn or missed a freeway exit. It was merely a coincidence that he and Ellen were on their way to a social function he had not wanted to attend.

Whether conscious or unconscious, Howard was able to regain some semblance of control, a sense of his own power and an outlet for his frustration by thwarting and frustrating his control-freak wife. His silences and dissent, forgetfulness and bungling only compelled Ellen to increase her efforts, but at least Howard was getting something out of the situation: vengeance.

Is There an Avenger in You?   If you tend to see controlling people as bad guys who set out with malice and forethought to make life difficult for you, then their control tactics may activate the avenger in you too. You would like to make them stop using those tactics on you altogether, but if you cannot, you'll settle for evening the score. You'll make them as miserable as they've made you or show them that you are in charge of something—even if it isn't remotely connected to the situation in which they got the upper hand. Maybe they can get to you and get their own way, but you can get back at them by:

- sulking, pouting or giving controllers the silent treatment.
- "forgetting" to return their calls, give them their messages, pick up the dry cleaning, or do anything else they expected you to do.
- withholding sex.
- talking behind their backs, going above their heads, spreading rumors, or otherwise stirring up trouble.
- bungling tasks they assign to you, making messes, accidentally losing or damaging their property or embarrassing them in front of people they are trying to impress.
- saying to yourself, "I don't get mad—I get even."

58

Rebellion

When Drew learned that Carl had used his influence to get him an interview with a prestigious medical group, he was furious. Carl had gone too far and Drew was going to make him see that. He was going to tell Carl exactly how he felt about his intrusions and interference, his sanctimonious suggestions and unsolicited advice.

Of course, he had told Carl off many times before. "I've talked till I'm blue in the face," Drew admitted. "If I've told him once, I've told him a hundred times, emergency medicine is what I do and the emergency room is where I'm going to stay. He just won't listen." And Drew was not going to give up. "If it's the last thing I do, I'll pound that message into Carl's thick head," he said.

Drew was a *rebel.* No one was going to tell him what to do or get away with trying to control him. Indeed, the mere possibility of being pushed around or manipulated instantaneously stirred up feelings of irritation, indignation and outrage. "How dare they?" were the first three words that ran through Drew's mind —quickly followed by "I'll show them." He proceeded to do just that, countering the controller's arguments point by point, throwing tantrums, making threats, issuing warnings, storming out of rooms, and slamming doors. Ironically, as he struggled to snatch back the reins of control and either prevent controllers from getting their way or convince them to see and do things his way, his behavior became virtually indistinguishable from that of a control freak.

Are You a Rebel? Rebellion is by far the most obvious form of resistance and it often appears to be worth the effort. Your anger gives you the impression that you are dealing from a position of strength and no one is going to call you a pushover. However, they might accuse you of cutting off your nose to spite your face. You often do just that when automatic, knee-jerk reactions to anyone who tries to control you cause you to strike back blindly and:

- refuse to listen or give credence to their advice—even though it might be sound and you might be able to benefit from it.

- snap at, criticize, denigrate or obliterate controllers, feeling that your hurtful words, unfair accusations and brutal character assassination are justified because "they started it."

- leave no stone unturned, reminding controllers of every other time they went too far in their efforts to get their own way.

- use more force than necessary, regretting your overreaction after the fact.

- think that you must have gotten through to someone once and for all only to find yourself in the same spot having the same argument over and over again.

59

Is Fighting Back Really Accommodating?

In some cases, it may not be. At certain times, or in certain situations, matching force against force may be necessary. If that's the case, and if you're willing to risk the possible consequences, then by all means fight.

Also, fighting back does help you feel more powerful, less out of control. No matter how your interactions turn out, you can take comfort from the fact that you didn't back down. You stood up for yourself. You gave those controllers a piece of your mind, maybe even got a few points across or enough zingers in to make them regret what they did to you.

But if you fight *automatically* whenever you're attacked, or every time someone tries to control you, you are almost certainly accommodating. Control freaks may not get as much from you as easily as they would if you automatically complied with their demands, but they still come out ahead.

In fight-back mode, you throw everything but the kitchen sink at controllers and they throw it all right back. You want to ward off their attack. They fight harder, or they retreat temporarily, then return to launch another attack from a different angle. You put up a good fight, but usually they outlast or outmaneuver you and end up getting what they were after anyway. Even when you come out ahead, they know their tactics got to you and next time will simply try harder. Win, lose, or draw, in the long run fighting back automatically will almost certainly cost you more effort than it's worth.

RECOGNIZING YOUR ACCOMMODATION STYLES

What is your most typical response to a controller? Do you tend to try to please, get even, keep the peace? This test can help you begin to see the automatic patterns you slip into when dealing with people who try to control you.

Rate each of these statements using the following scale:

1 = strongly disagree
2 = moderately disagree
3 = slightly agree
4 = moderately agree
5 = strongly agree

Peacekeeping

1. I'd rather give up what I want than have someone upset with me. _____
2. It's easier to get what I want if I make the other person think it's her/his idea. _____
3. I try to figure out what someone else wants and do it before s/he can become upset with me. _____
4. When someone I care about is angry with me, I'll do almost anything to get her/him to calm down. _____

TOTAL

People-Pleasing

5. I hate the "silent treatment" and will do almost anything to get someone to stop doing it. _____
6. What others think of me is very important. _____
7. I respond to criticism by trying to change whatever is "wrong." _____
8. When I think I might have offended someone, I bend over backward to make it up to her/him. _____

TOTAL

Self-Sacrifice

9. I do everything I can to avoid hurting other people. _____
10. I often get overloaded because I can't say no when I think someone needs my help. _____
11. When someone I care about asks me to do lots of things for her/him, I believe it only shows how much s/he needs me. _____
12. If someone at work seems overwhelmed, helpless or incompetent, I'll do her/his task myself—even if I'm already overloaded. _____

TOTAL

TOTAL OF ITEMS 1–12

Passive Resistance

13. When I'm upset with someone, I don't say anything but s/he gets the idea. _____

14. When someone is yelling at me, I won't give her/him the satisfaction of responding or even listening. _____

15. I often pretend I don't understand or know how to do something so a controller will stop asking me to do it. _____

16. When someone makes an unreasonable demand, I don't say no, but I take my own sweet time about doing it. _____

62

TOTAL

Retaliation

17. I get back at people who try to take advantage of me by giving them the silent treatment. _____

18. Sometimes I "forget" to do something just to see someone sweat it out her/himself at the last minute. _____

19. I tend to be more clumsy (spill or break things) around people who have a lot of power over me. _____

20. When I'm in a situation where I'm forced to do what someone else wants, I can usually find a way to get even. _____

TOTAL

Rebellion

21. When someone tries to make me do something, I refuse to do it—even if it's a good idea. _____

22. I lose my temper when someone tries to bully me, and often say or do things I regret later. _____

23. Even though I stand up to a controller, I find myself fighting the same battles over and over.

_____

24. I would rather stand up to a controller than be a wimp—even if I have to pay for it later.

_____

TOTAL

TOTAL OF ITEMS 13–24

Your Scores

A total possible score for each scale is 20. A score of 14 or more on any scale indicates that you probably rely on that pattern when responding to a controller. Comparing the total score of items 1–12 with that of items 13–24 will show you whether you typically use giving in or fighting back responses. If the scores are relatively even, you probably use both kinds of automatic responses, depending on the situation. Pay special attention to any single item rated 4 or 5.

63

Accommodation as Control

It's easy to see how fighting back tactics are really intended to control. Passive resisters hope the controller will get tired of all the maddening, indirect little roadblocks they can bring to bear. Avengers rely on the intimidation factor: "Those controllers better not mess with *me* if they know what's good for them!" (Actually, some avengers secretly hope the controller *will* mess with them—giving them a chance to get even.) These are the people who strut around saying, verbally or nonverbally, "Go ahead—make my day!" And, of course, rebels fight fire with fire—they like to meet the controller head on.

Giving in seems at first to be less controlling. But the give-in tactics we've described are actually forms of what social psychologists call "secondary (passive) control." Peacekeepers hope they can keep things sufficiently calm so that the control freak will feel no need to make a move. People-pleasers attempt to avoid control by keeping other people happy. Both groups commonly use empathy, personal sensitivity, and their ability to *anticipate* the controller's needs as countercontrol strategies. And, of course, self-sacrificers delay or forego getting their own needs met and keep as low a profile as possible to avoid the control freak's attack. Among other things, the tendency to use secondary control tactics may reflect both sex-role and cultural biases. On the average, women use secondary control more often than men. Individuals raised in Japan and other Asian cultures often tend to use secondary tactics, where Americans and Western Europeans seem to favor primary (aggressive) control.

At any rate, control begets control. Ultimately, we may become exactly what we are trying to avoid. In dealing with control freaks, we run the risk of *becoming control freaks ourselves*, trying to outmaneuver them just as hard as they try to control us. In the long run it amounts to the same thing and it doesn't do any of us any good.

64

Follow-up

Are you accommodating the controlling people in your life? Take out the scenario you wrote while examining your Achilles' heel in Chapter 2 and highlight or underline everything you did or said during that particular reaction. Then circle responses you *freely chose* to make after *consciously considering* your needs and your options. If you draw lots of circles on the page, congratulations. You're way ahead of most of us and may only need to polish up your communication skills (if that). But chances are that you won't be circling many responses. Most people operate on automatic at least some of the time when dealing with a control freak.

Now look over the responses you did not circle and answer the following questions:

1. What were you hoping that response would accomplish?
2. What did you actually accomplish?
3. What did the other person gain? Did you want to give that person what he or she wound up getting?
4. After you responded, did the other person try again or try harder to control you?

5. How did you feel about yourself and the situation after the fact? Were you proud of what you said or did? Did you wish you had responded differently? Did you feel dumb or embarrassed or ashamed of yourself?

6. What did your response say about you? Has the controlling person in your life used that information to his or her advantage at any time since that particular interaction took place?

7. How typical was your response? With what other people and under what other circumstances are you likely to use it? Can you remember when you started responding in that manner or why?

In the next chapter, we'll begin to explore in more detail some of the motives and payoffs that drive controllers—and accommodators—to behave the way they do.

65

MOTIVES AND PAYOFFS
WHY CONTROL FREAKS
AND ACCOMMODATORS
ACT THE WAY THEY DO

Mark is a thirty-six-year-old businessman for whom adjectives like arrogant, abrasive and overbearing are a perfect fit. He is a bull in the china shop of life, barreling through each day oblivious to the chaos he leaves in his wake. He has positive attributes, of course—keen intelligence, diverse interests, a quick-witted sense of humor. Generous as well, Mark sincerely wants to make people happy, to give them only the best. Unfortunately, even when Mark is being "good," he tends to go overboard.

"When we go out to dinner, he always asks the maître d' for the best table in the restaurant," said Mark's sister, Julie. "If, for any reason, he decides that the table we get isn't good enough, he makes a scene—arguing, asking to see the manager, saying, 'My sister drove a long way to have a pleasant, relaxing evening. I think she deserves better than this, don't you?' I'm mortified. I want the floor to open up and swallow me."

At every turn and at any cost, Mark goes all out to reach the goals he sets for himself. A "no" answer never stops him. He simply tries harder to turn it into a yes. Sometimes Mark's overpowering tactics are successful. But they are unsuccessful more often than you would expect, and with disquieting frequency they do Mark more harm than good.

For instance, a political group to which Mark belonged selected him along with several other members to represent the group at a national conference. Because space at the conference center was limited, delegates were not allowed to bring spouses or other guests. Naturally, Mark wasn't going to take that one lying down.

He called the delegation coordinator and presented a lengthy, impassioned argument as to why an exception to the "no spouse" rule should be made in his case. The coordinator denied Mark's request. Mark immediately dialed the group's president and presented the same argument to him with the same result. He then made several calls to people at national headquarters. When they also said no, Mark again called the delegation coordinator and delivered an ultimatum he was quite sure would convince Joe to do things his way.

"I won't attend the conference unless I can bring a guest," he said. But his control move backfired.

"Fine, I'll call the alternate," Joe replied and hung up.

Mark's controlling behavior was backfiring at work as well. In spite of his impressive real estate sales record, the partners in the firm were thinking about firing him. They had taken all they could take of his perpetual jockeying for position, lobbying for special treatment, and compulsion to ask for second, third and fourth opinions whenever he did not immediately get his own way.

67

Tracing the Source

I met Mark at a seminar designed to help sales managers deal with difficult employees. Mark quickly (almost proudly) acknowledged that most of the other registrants were probably at the seminar to learn to deal with people like *him*. But that afternoon, he said something touching and a little sad. "I wouldn't want to have me for an enemy! But I don't think I'd particularly want me for a friend, either."

When Mark was asked whether or not he thought his very aggressive style was getting him what he wanted out of life, he thought for a minute and then said, "Sometimes it does. I'm a good salesman, and I'm pretty successful in other ways. But sometimes I know I overreact, and it gets me in trouble. I've lost some business opportunities, a couple of girlfriends. A lot of people tell me I need to lighten up, keep a cork in it. I don't think I know how. That ol' cork just blows back on out." He shrugged. "I guess I was born this way."

Do you think Mark is right? Do some people come into the world genetically wired to be a pain in the neck? Is it an unchangeable characteristic, like blue eyes? Or is control-freak behavior learned? This is an important question, because most psychologists believe that anything that was learned can be at least partially unlearned.

Genetic or learned? The answer is probably a little bit of both. Some people may be born with a genetic predisposition to overcontrol, in the same way that, from day one, some babies are clearly more aggressive than others. This doesn't mean there is a control-freak gene that Mark and people like him can now blame for their outrageous behavior. No one really knows the extent to which genetic factors contribute to personality and behavioral styles. Evidence suggests there is a significant contribution; but Mark's tendency to insult waiters and embarrass his sister is probably more learned than inherited.

We will consider two questions in this chapter. First, to the extent that overcontrol patterns are learned, how are they learned? That is, how and why did Mark *start* being a control freak? The second question, basically, is, Why doesn't he *stop?* Given Mark's awareness that overcontrol often gets him in trouble, and the fact that he at least says he would like to develop other alternatives, what are the forces that keep him behaving the way he does? Why can't he change?

Learning to Be a Control Freak

Let's examine some of the ways Mark may have learned to be a control freak. These learning experiences begin early in life, and come from a variety of sources.

Controlling Behavior Works, Is Reinforced, and Becomes a Habit

At the age of six months, baby Mark wakes up alone. He is cold and wet, so he begins to cry. His mother is asleep on the couch and doesn't hear, so Mark cries louder. Still no response, so he screams. Mother wakes and rushes to comfort him; her presence and reassuring warmth calm him down and provide *powerful and immediate gratification* in direct response to his crying.

This is an example of what research psychologists call a "learning trial": stimulus (Mark feels discomfort), response (he cries), and reinforcement (his discomfort is reduced).

Sometime later, baby Mark is in the kitchen, in his high chair. He sees his bottle on the counter and points to it. Mommy, who is on the phone with her own mother, doesn't see, so Mark cries. Mommy turns around and says, "In a minute, honey." Mark squalls angrily and throws his strained spinach on the floor. Mommy thinks, "Oh, the heck with it—I want to finish this conversation." So she gives Mark his bottle. Mark gurgles happily. Stimulus, response, reinforcement.

The next two or three times Mark ups the ante to get something he wants, Mommy doesn't give in to his demanding cry—and eventually he calms down on his own. But then one night she is particularly tired, so she lets Mark sleep in her bed to stop his wailing. And next week, she is once again busy on the phone . . .

Mark's mother has her son on what researchers call an "intermittent reinforcement schedule." That is, she doesn't reward his controlling behavior every time he performs it, but rather every third, or fifth, or tenth time. As it turns out, in many situations intermittent reinforcement strengthens developing habits *better* than if the reward were given every time. New patterns take longer to learn when reinforced intermittently, but once learned, they become very difficult to break.

At this point, some of you may be thinking, Wait a minute! *All* mothers reward their kids for crying, at least some of the time. They can't help it. Why doesn't everyone grow up a raging control freak?

That is a question developmental psychologists have yet to unravel. A different child treated in precisely the same way as Mark might develop very different patterns. Some experts will tell you it has to do with genetics (the predisposition mentioned earlier); others believe that very early events in a child's experience most strongly influence how that child learns to react to later events and experiences. There are experts who will stress subtle and largely unconscious differences in the ways two mothers respond to their child's tears. And others might tell you that all this experiencing, responding, and reinforcing occurs within a particular *relationship* between mother and child. They would suggest that the nature of this relationship has a tremendous effect on how the reinforcement is interpreted.

There are other theories as well, and many of them have merit. But the bottom line is this: no one really knows. Most professionals agree that the way the mother responds to her child's demands has a major impact on the way that child develops; beyond that, it's open to debate.

Later in Childhood, Similar but More Complex Patterns Are Reinforced

Throughout his youth and young adulthood, Mark's skill at controlling people and events steadily improved. Indeed, it seemed to be rewarded and reinforced at every turn. His sister, Julie, did whatever he wanted if he bribed her with candy or threatened not to let her tag along with him and his friends. If he kept at his mother long enough or hit her with a ridiculous ultimatum like "I'll never speak to you again," she invariably gave in to his demands. Telling her how special and important their mother-son relationship was worked wonders as well. And many a teacher changed Mark's grades after he argued about the wording of a test question. Friends and relatives claimed that Mark could "sell ice cubes to an Eskimo," and Mark loved to hear that. He was becoming proud of the reputation his control skills had earned for him.

Because his parents rarely saw eye to eye on anything including their children's behavior, Mark inadvertently discovered that something forbidden by one parent would generally be allowed by the other. He used that knowledge to his advantage at every opportunity and became so adept at playing both ends against the middle that he almost never had to take no for an answer. Julie vividly remembered one particular occasion when Mark got away with murder by using this rudimentary control tactic.

"Mark was eight and Dad was recuperating from a heart attack," she recalled. "Mom made it very clear that we were *not*—under any circumstances—to go into Dad's bedroom without her. She made it sound like he would die if we did and that was enough of a threat to keep me in line. But not Mark." In retrospect, Julie surmised that Mark did not want to believe their father was as ill as their mother said he was. "I think he wanted to see with his own eyes that Dad was okay," she said. But whatever the reason, Mark—turning to the tactic that had worked for him so many times before—got around his mother's order by pleading his case to one of his father's nurses. Into Dad's room he went, and of course Dad was delighted to see him. Mom, who really was terrified of upsetting her husband, never did tell him about the subterfuge, so Mark got away clean.

Naturally Mark did not always get his way, but his control tactics worked often enough to convince him to keep using them. Again, control often works. Even when it produces negative side effects or long-term problems, the immediate result is success, gratification, a feeling of power, and, often, a mountain of "Attaboys!" (or "Attagirls!") from other people.

Adult Models Validate the Use of Control Tactics

Some of the most compelling lessons children learn are taught by role models—people whom they love, look up to or depend on and whose behavior they consciously or unconsciously emulate. Parents, relatives, teachers, media heroes, long-dead ancestors whose reputations are kept alive in stories passed from one generation to the next, or powerful peers—all can model behaviors the child unconsciously decided to make his own. Most often role models are parents whose constant contact with and emotional impact on their children make their every move a potential example of how to be . . . or not to be.

For instance, as a young girl, Ellen, the compulsive controller mentioned in previous chapters, was the apple of her father's eye. The mild-mannered, soft-spoken minister showered his eldest child with attention and affection whenever he was home. If he had spent more time with his family, perhaps Ellen would have adopted his good-natured, unassuming demeanor as her own. Unfortunately, because of his involvement in church business and community affairs, Ellen's father was not home very much. Even when he was, his unabashed adoration barely compensated for and certainly did not shield Ellen from the harsh treatment heaped upon her by her mother, a volatile, high-strung woman who demanded perfection from everyone she encountered.

Ellen never really understood why her father did not stand up to his wife. He said he didn't mind being bullied, because he knew his wife loved him and had his best interests at heart. Young Ellen was left with the impression that keeping a tight rein on everyone and everything around her was the proper

71

thing to do. So, even though she hated the way she and her father were treated, her mother's perfectionist standards and controlling behavior were what Ellen absorbed and carried with her into adulthood and into relationships like the one with her friend Beverly.

It is strange to think we sometimes model ourselves after parents and other figures *whose behavior we didn't even like.* But that is what happens. We may even say to ourselves, "Boy, I'm not going to treat my kids that way when *I* grow up!" But simultaneously, we see that behavior working for the adult—the controlling person clearly is coming out on top. At some level, with irrefutable childish logic, we must conclude, "Well, it's not okay to be *me* in this relationship—but it certainly seems okay to be *them.*" And off we go.

Alternatively, some children reject the behavior of a "weak" or "out of control" parent. "This is a bad way to be," they think, "so I will be the opposite." These unconscious decisions, made at a time when children lack the maturity, information or options to choose a different path for themselves, can have a tremendous influence on later behavior. We all learn from early role models, so if we are taking control to extremes today, chances are that at some level we are still paying homage to those early lessons.

Adults Tell Us How to Use Control Tactics

Everyone absorbs a great many instructional messages during childhood, swallowing them whole and automatically replaying them whenever circumstances warrant. The content of these messages differs from individual to individual, of course, causing different people to react to an identical situation in very different ways. (Four friends are walking on the beach in swimsuits. A voice behind them snickers, "Willya look at her! I didn't know the Goodyear blimp was back in town!" Janet thinks to herself, How sad that people have to say mean things to one another. Marcia gulps and thinks, Oh, God, I knew I should have worn my one-piece! Barbara mutters, "Blow it out your ear, garbagemouth!" And Linda looks at the sky, thinking, Where?)

Some people seem to have collected a great many internal messages that directly or indirectly encourage the use of control tactics:

- "Never leave anything to chance."
- "Be careful."
- "You should have known that would happen."
- "Just try harder."
- "Don't let them push you around."
- "You've got to show them who's in charge."
- "Can't you control yourself for two seconds?"
- "Everybody loves a winner, but they don't give the time of day to losers or quitters."

These messages as well as the treatment and the modeling we received from significant people in our lives shaped our perceptions of ourselves at various stages of development, and taught us how we should deal with the world around us.

73

Sometimes Role Models Become a "Part" of Us

Long after their ability to influence us directly has passed, role models can live on inside us in the form of inner voices, images, beliefs, values, and perspectives. Although they may not be appropriate or useful today, these patterns never really disappear from the scene. Indeed, the three-, five- or ten-year-olds who later became control freaks can still be said to exist as "inner children" within us adults—aspects of the personalities of significant figures on which we modeled our younger selves, and which now have the ability to pop out and become dominant under certain circumstances.

When a controller who could once get whatever she wanted from her mother by throwing a tantrum in a public place or in front of dinner guests reams out her kids or an employee in full view of other people, chances are that her inner child is steering the ship. Likewise, an inner child may be calling the shots when a controller who was discouraged from coming right out and asking for what he wanted pouts or hints around or uses other undermining tactics to get his own way.

A great deal has been written over the past couple of decades about how our "inner children" came to be the way they are, and the profound influence they can have on our lives. Among other things, this literature suggests that people with exceptionally controlling "inner children" tend to have been raised by:

- submissive parents who gave into them easily and often.
- competitive parents who encouraged them to outperform other children and not get pushed around.
- doting parents who placed them at the center of the universe and constantly told them how special they were.
- conditionally loving parents who promised their approval and acceptance for "good conduct" but expected perfection or upped the ante when their standards were met, compelling future control freaks to constantly try harder.
- childlike parents who abdicated their role, leaving the control freak to assume adult responsibilities at an early age.
- alcoholic or drug-addicted parents, who were unable to provide an environment of consistency, support, and loving direction.

74

Scratch beneath the surface of a control freak and the chances are you will find one or more of these patterns in his or her background.

Taking Control: The Struggle for Survival

Sadly, some children must deal on a daily basis with people and situations that are truly dangerous and that are totally outside both their understanding and their control. Research on adult children of alcoholics (ACAs) and on adult survivors of early abuse describe the extremes to which some children must go in order to survive.

The children of alcoholics and drug abusers typically must grow up fast, because there is no one else in the family who can function as a responsible adult. These kids virtually have no childhood. The circumstances of their lives—and even the way their parents will act from one minute to the next—are so unpredictable that they must constantly be on guard. In extreme cases, they may have to assume responsibility for the physical welfare of the entire family.

As bad as that may be, abused children have it even worse. Their very survival is in doubt. Ever vulnerable to physical and/or psychological attack, yet never knowing when or if that attack will come, their lives become an unpredictable hell. The only way some of these children can take "control" is to run, and the only place they can run to is deep inside themselves. So down inside they go, erecting protective walls and barricades—and sometimes alternative personalities or even entire realities—to shield themselves against the totally uncontrollable confusion and terror which exists in the outside world.

This is not to suggest that every ACA or adult survivor is a control freak. Many of them have control *issues,* but human development is not nearly that simple and straightforward. However, a large number of ACAs and adult survivors do seem to become controllers, accommodators, or both. Some do begin to exhibit control-freak behavior, and some develop accommodation habits that keep their adult lives almost as confusing and unpredictable as their childhoods had been. Ellen's upbringing is a perfect example.

Ellen's mother did more than display behavior for her daughter to emulate. She literally pounded her code of conduct into her, criticizing her unmercifully and pinching, slapping or severely punishing her for the slightest misdeed or error.

Avoiding that punishment quickly became Ellen's top priority. Indeed, from Ellen's youthful perspective, it seemed as if her sense of safety and security—her very survival—depended on figuring out exactly what her mother wanted and doing things exactly as her mother expected them to be done. Hoping to control the treatment she received, Ellen became very cautious, very careful and very determined to stay one step ahead of her mother.

The task Ellen had assigned herself became even more difficult to accomplish after her siblings were born. Inexplicably, her mother held her responsible for *their* misbehavior as well as her own. At some point Ellen concluded that she could protect herself from her mother's wrath only by keeping her brothers and sisters in line. By age twelve, she was not only running her own life with caution and care but also ordering her siblings around and taking over for them whenever she feared that they would fail to live up to her mother's expectations.

At least some of the time, Ellen's controlling behavior

worked and whenever it did, Ellen felt less helpless, less victimized by her mother, safer and more sure of herself in general.

Ellen had learned to cope by controlling, to make frightening, painful, unpredictable experiences feel less threatening by focusing her attention on other people or external events and trying with all her might to get them to conform to *her* expectations. Again, that's how many control freaks who were raised in dysfunctional families learned to survive. Desperately searching for a way to restore order to the chaos going on around them, they tried to control the dysfunctional person's behavior, to prevent their siblings from upsetting their parents or to assume their parents' roles and literally run their households.

Others coped with the loss of a loved one through death, divorce or abandonment by taking care of extraneous details. As adults, these are the people who become anxious or enraged when the smallest thing is out of place, the slightest detail left undone. Bullied and badgered by bigger or older youngsters, other future control freaks reacted by pushing around and picking on their smaller or younger playmates. Still others bragged or sweet-talked their way into the spotlight in order to feel less out of place in a new school or neighborhood.

Although the exact nature of their experiences and the tactics they used to cope may vary, controlling behavior did, at one time, help many control freaks and accommodators survive, emotionally and/or physically. The importance of staying in control became permanently etched in their minds. Now the mere thought of dealing with stressful or challenging circumstances in any other way can leave them feeling as anxious or threatened as they felt during childhood (or whenever the painful experiences originally occurred). Naturally, they cope with those distressing present-day emotions the same way they coped with them in the past—by taking control.

These are some of the factors that contribute to the development of a control freak. Now it's time to consider our second question: What are the forces that keep controllers and accommodators behaving the way they do? And for people like Mark, who at least say they would like to develop other alternatives, why is overcontrol such a hard habit to kick?

Staying a Control Freak

Control freaks *believe* in control. They have spent years and years proving to themselves that holding on to the reins is the most effective way to operate. On a rational level they may be aware their control habit is doing them more harm than good. But the belief in control is still hard to shake. You see, many control freaks (along with many of the rest of us) commit a logical fallacy that makes their ideas about control very difficult to question. Read the story in the accompanying box to get an idea of how this fallacy operates.

KEEPING THE INDIANS AWAY

A certain man spent each morning sitting on his roof tearing newspaper into little pieces and throwing them into the wind. One day, a neighbor came over and asked him what he was doing. "I'm keeping the Indians away," the man replied. "That's crazy! There are no Indians around here!" the neighbor exclaimed. "See?" said the man as he began mutilating the sports section. "It works!"

This man's theory about how to keep Indians away *cannot be disproved as long as he keeps using it successfully.* And he is too afraid of Indians to stop. (By the way, this guy looks like a nut only to people who don't believe there is an Indian problem. Everyone else on the block hires him as a consultant.)

Control freaks overcontrol in order to keep the Indians away. If they would only stop throwing paper off the roof long enough to see whether or not there are really Indians out there, they might be very pleasantly surprised. But, like the fellow in the story, most controllers are too afraid of arrow wounds to take that chance.

Beyond an unshakable belief in control, there are five major incentives, or payoffs, that help keep control freaks in the game. Controlling helps them:

1. meet their needs.
2. ward off their fears and prevent catastrophes.

3. fulfill their expectations.

4. stay a part of their current "system."

5. *feel* in control of their own lives.

Understanding how these payoffs work will help you deal with controllers more effectively than you have in the past. In the remainder of this chapter, we'll take a closer look at each and give you a chance to identify the ones that may be motivating the controlling people in your life.

Control Delivers

Control behavior works well enough and often enough to help controllers satisfy their needs in a variety of ways.

Tangible Payoffs Cassie wanted Sam to accept her photo assignment and he did—after she launched into an angry tirade, overpowering him with furious accusations of disloyalty and ingratitude. She had controlled, and control delivered.

Irene wanted to know what the public relations staff was doing at all times. So she led various staff members to believe that she was sharing confidential information with them (and only them), expressed her concerns about another employee and asked her "confidants" to keep an eye on that person. With her network of spies regularly reporting back to her, Irene was able to stay on top of everything that happened in her department. She had controlled, and control delivered.

Carl wanted his son Billy to drop the woman he had been seeing. So Carl tirelessly lectured Billy, forbade him from bringing "that gold digger" to family gatherings, silenced other family members when they discussed her in his presence and adamantly refused to refer to his son's girlfriend by name. Several months after Carl instituted his campaign, Billy's relationship ended. Carl had controlled. Although his efforts may have had nothing to do with the demise of his son's relationship, Carl still got what he wanted. Control appeared to deliver—and that is close enough to count for most control freaks.

As mentioned earlier, control can and often does deliver, producing tangible results that are the most obvious incentives for continuing to use controlling behavior. Control also delivers results that are invisible to the naked eye, fulfilling internal needs, desires and wishes even when it appears that no external end has been accomplished.

Intangible Payoffs   The need to verify or enhance their self-image is a powerful incentive for many controllers, especially those who already view themselves as confident, competent human beings. Their rather lofty opinion of themselves supports their contention that things work better when they are in charge and their belief that, by virtue of their superior intellect, skill or position, they are entitled to get their own way. Each time they successfully control you, control freaks confirm their perceptions and boost their egos.

Controlling behavior may also fulfill a need for respect, power or achievement. A desire to impress you or a third party (their boss, for example, or your parents) may also motivate control freaks. Or they may wish to be heard—and to hear from you that they have gotten through. Sometimes control freaks want attention or praise for taking care of details that other people overlook. At other times they are after vindication, perhaps even revenge. (You made me angry and kept me from getting what I wanted, they think. You had no right to do that and I have the right to get even or make sure you don't do it again.) And sometimes control freaks control for the sheer pleasure of it. Simply sensing that they are in control makes them feel terrific. They are excited and full of energy whenever they are calling the shots.

Whether controllers are knowingly striving to achieve a tangible goal or instinctively attempting to meet their needs, *actually obtaining* that outcome produces a powerful side effect, a positive emotional "rush" that can be even more reinforcing than the outcome itself. Their practical or psychological success once again confirms control freaks' long-held belief that they can get whatever they want by controlling and that they *should* be in control. But more importantly, as they close the gap between a need and its fulfillment, a desire and its satisfaction, or a wish and its realization, they feel tremendous gratification. All is well in their world and they are safe, secure and in charge of their own lives.

Control Protects

While watching the evening news, Emma, the guilt-inducing mother mentioned in Chapter 1, went into a tailspin. She heard a weatherman say, ". . . hurricane moving up the coast . . ." and began to pace. She changed channels only to see more weather maps with multicolored hurricane symbols on them. Frantically, she telephoned her daughter, Lisa. "Do you think I should have the out-of-town guests come in a day early?" she asked. "We could put them up in hotels. We have to do *something* or that damn hurricane will ruin *my* wedding."

Of course it was Lisa's wedding, not Emma's. But Emma had made it her top priority from the moment Lisa and her fiancé, Jack, announced their engagement. "She went completely overboard trying to control every last detail," Lisa recalled. "She worried constantly. About everything under the sun."

Emma worried about making the "right" impression on the wedding guests, many of them socially prominent associates of her husband, a lawyer and powerful talent agent. She went so far as to call all of Jack's relatives just to make sure that they would dress appropriately for the black tie affair—offending many of them in the process. Emma worried about potentially embarrassing breaches of etiquette. When her son's wife RSVP'd using a word processor instead of sending a handwritten note, she became convinced that her daughter-in-law would end up humiliating her and threatened to take her off the guest list—a move which instigated a family argument that lasted for weeks.

Feeling that she just couldn't trust the bridal party to be where they were supposed to be when they were supposed to be there, Emma began sending out itineraries two weeks before the wedding. But she changed them so often that the bridesmaids and ushers did not know which note beginning with "Please disregard my previous note" they actually should disregard.

"Mom said that she was only trying to plan a wedding that would be perfectly wonderful in every way," Lisa commented. "But her obsession with making sure nothing went wrong was driving everyone crazy. And that hurricane thing. That was really nuts. All the forecasts said it would hit land three hundred miles to the east the day *after* the wedding!"

Protection Has Its Price   Emma derived no discernible pleasure from her constant nagging, worrying, reminding and controlling. The little she did accomplish was overshadowed by the trail of offended, furious and frustrated people she left in her wake. Yet her paralyzing fear of what might happen if she loosened her grip and the catastrophes she imagined occurring if she did not act to prevent them compelled her to continue controlling. "Everyone kept telling me to lighten up and relax," she said. "I tried. I really did. But I couldn't stop thinking of things that could go wrong. And once those thoughts got into my head, I just *had* to do something about them."

Like Emma, many control freaks control *defensively*—to prevent something they dread and to protect themselves from the consequences they fear they will suffer if they do not remain in control. Controlling behavior is an integral part of their psychological survival system. Triggered by real, imaginary, immediate or anticipated threats to their physical or emotional well-being, an alarm goes off in the control freak's mind. A warning message—"You're in for it now. You'd better do something *fast*"—rides in on a wave of anxiety. We all receive that message in situations that threaten us and we all react defensively to it. Control freaks believe that the best defense is control.

Insecurity and Self-Doubt Some people switch to control mode when they fear that they will be hurt, rejected, abandoned, ridiculed, criticized, ignored or disappointed by others. Even when they appear cool, calm and confident, many control freaks are plagued with feelings of insecurity and self-doubt. As a friend put it, they are "egomaniacs with inferiority complexes," who control to compensate for low self-esteem.

Some fear, as Emma did, that they are inherently flawed or deficient, not good enough in general and certainly not as competent as other people appear to be. Controlling you may be their only source of positive feelings about themselves. They may compete with and try to stay one up on you to prove to themselves that they are not losers. Getting you to agree with them or comply with their demands may counteract their fear that their opinions, decisions, feelings and interpretation of events are silly or worthless. And, of course, if they hold on to the reins of control tightly enough, they may even be able to conceal their presumably fatal flaws and glaring inadequacies from you.

Fear of Losing Control The fear of losing control can also be a powerful motivator. Such people feel that if they do not

81

control themselves, if they allow themselves to get upset, they might start crying and never stop, become angry enough to injure or even kill someone, have a breakdown and end up in a mental institution, or simply be overwhelmed by their guilt, shame or pain. So they control their own feelings and behavior with a tight rein; and, just so there are no surprises, they try to control yours as well.

Finally, the controllers in your life may be afraid of *being* controlled. If such a catastrophe were to occur, they might be forced to do things they did not want to do. They might be used, abused, taken advantage of, or burdened with more responsibilities than they can handle. Convinced that their best defense is a good offense, they try to control other people before other people can control them.

Responding to fear and anxiety by trying to control people and circumstances *appears* to get the job done. In paying attention to what is going on around them rather than what is happening inside, control freaks are able to reduce their feeling of anxiety and fear. They may not have solved their problems. They may have made matters worse. But they feel relieved and reassured nonetheless. This perception that they are back in the driver's seat and out of danger is very, very reinforcing—virtually guaranteeing that they will turn to their control tactics for self-protection again and again and again.

Control Fits

Most of us become control freaks from time to time. However, there are people whose personalities seem tailor-made for the part. Naturally inclined to run the show and appearing to have been born with the ability to do just that, they are take-charge types who seem to feel the urge to control more powerfully and more often than the rest of us. Kim's friend Alan certainly did.

Alan was a classic overachiever whose life revolved around an intense striving to attain the personal and professional goals he set for himself. He was forever moving forward, never standing still. There was always one more mountain to climb and he raced through each day trying to reach the next peak. He walked, talked, ate and thought at a breakneck pace and rarely did only one thing at a time.

Impatient and incapable of just relaxing and doing nothing, Alan had little tolerance for incompetence, delays or unforeseen circumstances that bollixed up his jam-packed schedule or prevented him from getting to every item on his lengthy "to do" lists. He couldn't stop himself from urging other people to move faster or from interrupting people to express his point of view.

Alan was a control freak. Anyone who knew him would tell you that. He accused his secretary of being completely incompetent each time she made a typographical error. His colleagues watched meetings drag on for hours while Alan and another equally controlling partner in the law firm insisted on "discussing" a point until one conceded that the other was right. And Kim, got pushed around by him constantly, like the long line of similarly timid, insecure and somewhat sheltered women who preceded her. He considered himself an expert on everything from how much makeup women should wear to how dishes should be stacked in a dishwasher and painstakingly instructed Kim on how to do these and many other things. He launched into condescending monologues or furious tirades at the slightest provocation and Kim often felt as if she were "walking through a minefield or working the high wire without a net."

Yet Alan wasn't being malicious, intentionally. He was simply being himself: a capable, successful, achievement-oriented person who saw himself as eminently qualified—and therefore obligated—to take charge of any situation and give other people the benefit of his knowledge and experience whether they wanted it or not. To Alan, life was about accomplishing things, about making things happen and control was part of the process, something that came as naturally to him as breathing. It *fit* him like a glove.

Control also fits:

- *Perfectionists,* who think, If only you, I and everything around us were the way I believe they should be, then I would be happy. They control in hope of fulfilling their impossibly high expectations and preventing everyone, including themselves, from making mistakes.

- *Obsessive-compulsive individuals,* whose lives revolve around cleaning, handwashing, counting, checking or other rituals and who control in response to their overwhelming need to maintain order and stick to their routines.

- *Narcissists,* who treat people as if they were objects that

83

exist only to please them and feed their sense of self-esteem. They control to ensure that other people's behavior reflects positively on them.

- *Addicts,* whose top priority is their "supply," the substance or activity that produces their high. They control to get their supply, to keep it, and to make sure that you don't stop them from using it.

- *"Type A" personalities,* who are driven by chronic, low-grade hostility and a sense of time-urgency. They get angry at the slightest provocation, and tend to control others "to make damn sure nothing like that ever happens again!"

- *Codependents,* who desperately need to control the addicts in their lives in a whole variety of ways.

84

Of course, individuals need not fit into a specific category or qualify for a psychiatric label to be predisposed to control. Control behavior may simply fit particularly well with their view of themselves, other people, the world around them, and their beliefs about how best to stay alive and get things done.

Many controllers view the world as a dangerous place full of hostile, unpredictable people who are only out for themselves. So they make sure to keep their guard up at all times and act before anyone can move in and prevent them from getting their own way. Others see the world and everyone in it as existing only for their benefit. Placing themselves at the center of the universe, they are convinced that anything they want should be given to them.

The controller in your life may have a mental picture of relationships, perhaps believing that someone who loves him will want to fulfill his needs. Truly feeling unloved when his demands are not met, he tries harder and harder to compel you to meet them. Or your controlling boss, mother, daughter or wife may view relationships as a delicately balanced system of debits and credits. That person may act as if you owe her compliance because she hired, befriended, married or gave birth to you, did favors for you in the past, or simply because she never rejected you.

Everyone strives to maintain the stance he or she feels most comfortable taking. If someone says, "I've always been the strong one," he is probably describing a role he held and grew accustomed to in his family or in other relationships. You can bet he feels most comfortable when he is in charge, making decisions or handling crises, and that he will choose self-determination over interdependence or collaboration no matter what he may say to the contrary. Likewise, someone who has "always been a fighter" will feel most comfortable when engaged in some sort of battle or competition; she will view people as adversaries to be beaten or obstacles to be removed from the battlefield. And there almost certainly will be people in her life who not only support that viewpoint, but enthusiastically cheer her on as she moves forward into the fray.

Control as Part of a System

The sad truth is that control-freak behavior doesn't occur in a vacuum. As much as we may complain about the controllers in our lives, at another level many of us rely on these people to come through for us, to get the job done in ways uniquely suited to their controlling style. You see, control behavior doesn't just "deliver" for the control freak. It delivers for *those of us who rely* on control freaks as well.

85

Consider the college football coach who rules his team with an iron hand and will do virtually anything to field a winning squad. He treats his players like eight-year-olds, breaks every recruitment rule in the book, and after losing a game has bodily thrown reporters out of the locker room. In addition it is generally known, though not advertised, that he verbally abuses his players, and occasionally abuses them physically as well. At home he is no different—he bosses his wife around, screams at TV football games, and once dislocated his son's shoulder when, during an argument, the boy tried to leave the room without permission.

This man is a diehard control freak, and everyone knows it. Colleagues and students alike deplore his coaching tactics, not to mention his clear emphasis on winning over sportsmanship, honesty, ethics, scholastics or anything else. They believe he provides a bad role model for his athletes, is not an acceptable school representative (except on the football field), and has values that would shame Attila the Hun.

Will this man be quietly relieved of his responsibilities, asked to turn in his locker key, and referred to a qualified therapist? Not likely. The team is winning and there is a Bowl bid on the horizon. Wealthy alumni are contributing large sums of money that support needed educational programs, and the new TV contract is going to help build a chemistry laboratory. On Saturday afternoon, eighty thousand fans cram into the stadium and cheer loudly enough to wake the dead—and some of them are the very same people who criticize the coach most vehemently during the week.

The coach is trapped. He knows only one way to get the job done—by kicking butt and taking names. He is reviled for it on the one hand but honored and rewarded on the other. If, for some reason, he stopped being a control freak for a week, everyone would think he was sick. And if he stopped permanently, he would probably be fired, because his team's performance would suffer. Other coaches might be able to field a championship team without resorting to control-freak behavior. But not this fellow, he simply doesn't know how.

None of us is an island. We are all part of very complex social networks and systems. The ways we behave, interact, and produce are also part of that system. Now, systems theorists tell us that when a significant change occurs in one area, the entire system is thrown out of balance. According to the principle of homeostasis, the system will *try to rebalance itself*, that is, either reverse the original change or make new changes that will return the system to balance and harmony. New changes are difficult to make, so the system first will try to reverse the original change, *even if that change was a positive one.*

In other words, control-freak behavior is not maintained solely by the fears, needs, and priorities of the control freak. The needs and expectations of the people around him or her may have a big effect as well. The very people who most deplore the control freak's ways may, at another level, be working as hard as they can to keep him or her from changing. This apparent contradiction might seem strange, but in fact it is extremely common—family therapists in particular deal with it on a daily basis.

For example, it may be that as much as Lisa hates Emma's worrying every little wedding detail to death, she also *relies* on her mother to make sure nothing goes wrong. Lisa might not agree, might even be offended by such a suggestion—but Emma certainly has performed that function for her daughter in the past. And it is a good bet that if Emma ever pulled out of the wedding plans, Lisa would be the one to panic.

Control as an End in Itself

The fifth incentive for control-freak behavior is the very feeling of being in control which that behavior produces. Many controllers are hooked on it. The heady rush of power, the tremendously gratifying sense that they are making things happen (even if they really aren't), and the feelings of relief and reassurance they experience from simply *trying* to control are extremely pleasurable. The thought of not feeling that way (or worse yet, feeling controlled or out of control) is extremely distressing—so much so that any and all negative consequences that ensue as a result of their controlling behavior seem insignificant. Indeed, control freaks are willing to pay in pain and misery, sacrificing their long-term goals, hurting people they love and doing untold damage to their relationships, in order to maintain even the *illusion* of control.

The Illusion of Control For some individuals, actual outcomes don't seem to matter very much. The illusion of control is more than enough to produce the high which they find so compelling. In fact, *controllers sometimes confuse the feeling their controlling behavior creates with actually being in control.* Mark certainly did. Even though nearly every move he made backfired, he sincerely believed and would be the first one to tell you that he had everything under control. He wasn't being stupid or stubborn. He hadn't consciously decided that he would rather be right than happy or would rather end up with 100 percent of nothing than compromise to get 50 or 75 percent of something. His control habit had become an addiction, a powerful craving which he would go to any lengths and pay any price to satisfy. If people you know seem to control as an end in itself rather than as a means to an end, chances are they are control addicts too. Their addiction makes understanding them and coping with their behavior difficult—but not impossible.

What Good Does It Do to Know Why?

Once you begin to understand some of the motives that underly control-freak behavior, you may be able to stop taking that behavior quite so personally. You will realize that no matter how it may seem, most of the time control freaks aren't really out to *get* you. Their behavior primarily reflects *their* needs, *their* fears, *their* expectations; you just happen to be in the firing line. Sometimes this may seem like small consolation, and it certainly does not give them the right to boss you around, manipulate your feelings, or in any way reduce the quality of your life. But seeing control-freak behavior as a habit or need rather than as a personal attack may help you react to it more objectively, and will be of great help as you attempt to deal with control tactics more effectively.

In addition, once you can make an educated guess about the incentives for someone's controlling behavior, you can begin to help that person meet his needs, ward off his fears, fulfill his expectations or feel in control *without* sacrificing your own needs in the process. That is the essence of the harmonious, collaborative relationships which subsequent chapters of this book will help you learn to attain.

Follow-up

In the meantime, return to the scenario you prepared while completing the exercise at the end of Chapter 2. Read it over and then answer the following questions:

1. What tangible results do you think the person who tried to control you was after? What intangible needs, wants or wishes might he or she have been trying to fulfill? (You don't need to be a mind reader; just make your best guess.)

2. What real, imagined, immediate or anticipated dangers do you think that person was trying to avoid? What might he or she have been afraid of?

3. How did that person's actions fit his or her personality? What notions, beliefs or expectations might have influenced his or her approach to that situation or decision to control you?

4. Were there other people or circumstances which may have influenced that person's attempt to control you?

Might behaving differently have caused the controller other problems?

5. Do you suspect that he or she was more interested in feeling in control than in actually controlling you or the outcome of your interaction? What led you to that conclusion?

Think about several other recent experiences with controlling people and answer the same five questions. Your increasing ability to find the incentives behind controlling behavior will come in handy when you have learned a few new skills and are ready to respond to control freaks in more effective ways.

Control Traps

89

Whether you give in or fight back, when you favor a certain behavioral style and practice it over and over again, it becomes a habit. You begin to have a great deal of trouble doing anything else, even though the pattern in question may not be working for you at all. Hooked on accommodation, you may find yourself involved with control freaks in a variety of settings. But, naturally, the very worst problems occur between you and that controlling "significant other" in your life—your control-freak spouse, parent, child, boss, lover or friend.

People involved in long-term control relationships tend to develop repetitive and oddly compatible patterns of moves and countermoves which stabilize and become very difficult to break, or even to understand. Carefully observing such relationships will reveal, on the one hand, individuals who clearly want to get their needs met, avoid serious pain or harm, and generally maximize the quality of their lives. Ask them, that's what they'll tell you.

But on the other hand, you will see these people dealing with one another in ways that, in the long run, *couldn't possibly lead to a positive outcome for anyone.* The games they play, the things they say and do, would seem absolutely insane to anyone who hasn't had similar experiences him- or herself. And many (though not all) of the participants themselves will be all too aware of how destructive their relationships really are. If you asked them, they might defend or deny or explain—but in their hearts they know. Further, they *know* they have to make a change. Yet somehow they can't bring themselves to do so. That's why we call these crazy, self-propagating patterns *control traps.*

For instance, Kim, who saw herself as uneducated, unsophisticated and possibly unworthy of her relationship with Alan, put him on a pedestal and deferred to him whenever he tried to influence her thoughts, feelings and actions. She got into the habit of giving her power away and once she had, it was extremely difficult to get it back. Always able to come up with what she believed were excellent reasons for letting Alan control her, Kim became so adept at justifying both her own and Alan's actions that she easily talked herself out of asserting herself in any way.

"Every so often I'd get fed up with living under a dictatorship," Kim explained. "I'd muster up enough nerve to confront Alan. But then, just when I was about to put my foot down, he'd do something incredibly sweet or sensitive like treat my entire family to a weekend at Lake Tahoe or get tickets to a show he knew I really wanted to see or help me solve a problem I was having at work." Kim would think, I can't give him a hard time now, not when he just did this terrific thing for me, and she would swallow her feelings and postpone her protest once again.

Of course, whatever Alan had done did not make up for the verbal abuse he had heaped upon Kim in the past. It did not mean he would push her around any less in the future. But Kim's urge to accommodate Alan was just too strong. She had no more control over it than Alan had over his urge to control Kim. She used his sweetness as a *reason* to back off. And so, both Kim and Alan continued to behave true to form.

Alan gave directions. Kim followed them. He adopted the role of teacher and quizzed her. She played the part of good student and told him whatever she thought he wanted to hear. Alan criticized just about anything Kim said or did. Kim began to consider Alan's probable reaction before saying or doing almost anything, and adapted her behavior accordingly. He controlled. She accommodated. And they both made their moves and countermoves so automatically and predictably that their interactions might as well have been scripted for them ahead of time.

Whether Kim was actually swayed by Alan's control tactics or merely pretended to be, each time she engaged in her typical self-effacing, peacekeeping behavior, she confirmed Alan's belief that he was an exceptionally knowledgeable, sophisticated and powerful person who was entitled and perhaps even obligated to tell other people what to do. Since that was the perception that fueled his controlling behavior and Kim unwittingly reinforced it, Alan was all the more motivated to do what he was already inclined to do.

Each time he did, Kim was reminded of her own "less than" status, confirming *her* original belief that she was not very smart, competent, lovable or deserving and could not disagree with or upset other people if she wanted to be loved and accepted by them. Since that was the perception that activated her programming and Alan repeatedly reinforced it, Kim was unlikely to alter her responses in any way.

Because Alan's domination triggered Kim's submissiveness and her submission fed into his desire to dominate her, they both continued to do what they had always done since the beginning of their relationship. They were frozen in time, caught in a vicious cycle of control moves and accommodating countermoves which Kim had begun to pay for with migraine headaches and anxiety attacks. Unless one of them chose to change or unless something extraordinary happened, the pattern was likely to repeat itself indefinitely. And altering a control relationship such as Kim's and Allan's is no easy task.

When an accommodator does try to change, the controller will typically try (directly and/or indirectly) to undermine that change, and return the situation to the way it was. If the controller succeeds in reactivating the accommodator's old patterns, he will sigh with relief and the twosome will go another round. However, the controller will now be aware that his power is waning, and may up the ante, trying even harder to rule with an iron hand or using more subtle and sophisticated strategies to keep his partner down. The accommodator, having had a brief taste of freedom (which she almost certainly found to be a mixed blessing), will respond in kind. The result is often an even more destructive, unpleasant situation than had existed before.

Teacher/Student

At any rate, Kim and Alan had fallen into a pattern that is all too common in romantic relationships. Because it so closely resem-

91

bles the relationship between Eliza Doolittle and Henry Higgins in Shaw's play *Pygmalion*, it is known as the "Pygmalion complex." Some call it more simply the "teacher/student trap."

In the general case, know-it-all controllers bestow their wisdom on timid, insecure accommodators who endlessly try to change themselves into the people they think the controllers want them to be. Unfortunately, as was the case with Kim and Alan, what the teacher *really* wants is a perpetual student. In order to keep his student in that role, he must either *undermine her every attempt to significantly benefit from his teaching*, or continually up his standards to higher and higher levels of perfection.

Although teacher/student relationships can go on for years, eventually they nearly always dissolve. If the student does learn to function on her own, she "graduates," leaving her teacher for a more balanced relationship. If she doesn't, the teacher eventually tires of her, "flunks her out," and goes off to find a fresh, new student.

Although you may not be caught in the teacher/student trap, one of the following may ring a bell.

Caretaker/Wounded Bird

Here, cloyingly helpful controllers give intrusive, unsolicited advice and assistance to winsome, wistful accommodators who believe they cannot take care of themselves (or don't want to have to try). Wounded birds allow other people to assume responsibility (and take the blame) for their lives. Caretakers, of course, keep a running tally of their good deeds. Should their helpfulness fail to control the wounded bird, they cash in their chips for guilt to use as added leverage. If wounded birds begin to recover from their terminal dependency, controllers may fall apart themselves in order to maintain the upper hand.

Screw-up/Martyr

This is the reverse of the caretaker/wounded bird pattern. Whining, complaining, hopelessly ineffective controllers surround themselves with self-sacrificing accommodators and play round after round of a game psychiatrist Eric Berne called "Schlemiel/Schlamazel." Screw-ups forget, lose things, bungle routine tasks, or bombard martyrs with "dumb" questions. Martyrs want to wring their necks, but don't because they have been bamboozled into thinking that the screw-ups didn't mean to or couldn't help doing what they did. The screw-up apologizes. The martyr forgives. The screw-ups proceed to screw up some more and martyrs begin to handle things for them—which is precisely the outcome the bumbling controller was after in the first place.

Warden/Inmate

Here we find powerful, punitive controllers who have inflexible expectations for the people in their lives. They throw tantrums, sulk, pout, withhold sex, give lectures and otherwise mete out sentences to "inmates" who violate their rigid code of conduct. Prisoners complain that if it weren't for the warden they would be able to do all sorts of things—things they are actually afraid to do or think they could not succeed at if they tried to do them. Although they claim to be miserable, inmates do nothing to improve their lot and justify their inaction by pointing out the fact that their wardens are forcing them to stay in the same situation. By preventing them from facing their fears or feelings of inadequacy, wardens are actually doing inmates a favor while fulfilling their own expectations.

Superhero/Ingrate

Superheros are played by controllers with an overly developed sense of responsibility who believe they are indispensable, or fear that something terrible will happen if they are not in charge. They take on dozens of fatiguing and conflicting obligations ostensibly for the benefit of ingrates—the people they are actually trying to control. Then when they want to keep other people in line or get them to do their part to implement their plans, superheroes call in the "favors" ingrates never asked them to do in the first place, reminding them that they are running themselves ragged for *"your* benefit, not mine."

If all else fails, they collapse under the weight of all the burdens they have taken on, making ingrates feel guilty enough to give them their way. Ingrates usually feel as if they are *supposed* to be grateful or *should* be doing more. They may also believe they couldn't get along without the superhero's help. Thus, they fall for the superhero's ploys time and time again.

Abuser/Victim

This is one of the most malignant types of control traps. It involves controllers who inflict physical or emotional pain on relatively defenseless accommodators who either cannot or will not do anything to extract themselves from the situation. Among other things, abusers get a scapegoat on whom to vent their rage and frustration. Victims get what at some level they think they deserve, and/or they use their situation as an excuse not to examine or change their own lives. In their helpless, downtrodden state, they can see no alternatives, and believe they have no place else to go.

Righteousness

The "righteousness trap" is created by two or more people who seemingly would rather be right than happy. (As stupid as it sounds, this is an amazingly easy trap to fall into. Have you ever found yourself getting into an argument with a spouse, parent or teenager that you *knew* was not going to solve anything and, in addition, was probably going to wind up ruining your evening, or worse? A little internal voice was screaming at you, "Let it go, it's not worth it!" but you went ahead and did it anyway? That's what it feels like to choose being "right" over being "happy."

This pattern most often results from a matchup between a control freak and a rebel or a passive resister. Both want to come out on top and get their own way, and will sacrifice almost anything to do so. Throwing out the baby with the bath water is second nature to these folks. They will gladly fight to the death for 100 percent of nothing rather than compromise to get 50 or 75 percent of something. Their relationships are riddled with repetitive and escalating win-lose conflicts—in which one person gets what he wants at the other's expense—or lose-lose conflicts—in which each person makes sure the other does not get what he is after even if that means sacrificing what he wants himself.

Final Thoughts

These are just a few of the many ways people can get ensnared in difficult, unrewarding control patterns. The list could go on and on. Actually, there are as many control traps as there are controllers and accommodators, for every relationship is unique.

By now you may have some ideas regarding your own control-accommodation patterns. Specifically:

- who in your life regularly and repeatedly tries to control you

- how they get to you and what psychological incentives motivate them to use those tactics on you

- how you automatically respond and unwittingly make it easier for controllers to receive the payoffs they are after or encourage them to try harder to control you

- how, over time, these patterns of control, accommodation, and counter-control fuse into systems that are self-propagating and very, very difficult to break

95

The following has been said before, but bears repeating. Controller/accommodator interactions are so complex that you practically need a scorecard to tell controllers from controllees and a guidebook to distinguish control moves from accommodating ones. While who does what to whom is significant, *both* the controller and the accommodator do their parts to keep control patterns going. The result is seemingly unresolvable conflicts, decreases in productivity, and perpetual frustration. In the long run, nobody really wins.

Nonetheless, because the accommodator is the person who is regularly and repeatedly subjected to someone else's control tactics, *the accommodator usually suffers more.* Productivity is impaired as stress takes a heavy toll, and the symptoms are not subtle. Tension headaches, backaches, upset stomachs, insomnia, overeating or drinking, and other signs of chronic stress may be present. Do you take tranquilizers? How do you rate your self-esteem? Victims of control traps frequently feel disgusted with themselves and tell themselves how stupid, weak-willed or inept they are for allowing themselves to be treated so badly.

It is a hard fact of the control dynamic that even when they are alienating everyone around them and running themselves ragged, control freaks usually derive more satisfaction from controlling you than you derive from accommodating them. Moreover, the longer they play the game, the easier it becomes for them. After a while, all a skilled control freak needs to do is

signal (with a raised eyebrow, slammed door or moment of silence) that she is about to make a move. You, the accommodator, will stand up and salute.

On the other hand, as time goes on, you may be forced to
escalate your accommodating behavior, doing more to get less.
For instance, during the early years of their friendship, Beverly
changed her behavior whenever Ellen criticized. But now, anticipating criticism, she tries to second-guess Ellen and behave in
the way she thinks is most likely to please her. This requires
more energy (and skill) on Beverly's part and still leads to criticism when she guesses wrong.

Over the long haul, you begin to mistrust your own perceptions and doubt your own abilities. Your self-esteem begins to
plummet. You find yourself cast in the role of the loser who
never seems to get what he wants, or the victim who constantly
gets what he does not want. Yet, you continue to accommodate,
because at some level the positive payoffs are still there.

96

Follow-up

Drawing upon the information you found in this chapter, ask
yourself what payoffs might be perpetuating your accommodating response patterns (and in turn, a controller's controlling behavior). *What are you getting from relating to the controlling
people in your life the way that you do?* Are you avoiding risks
or responsibility? By letting other people control you, do you
save yourself the embarrassment of making mistakes or the hassle of making decisions? Do you get to blame the person in control when things go badly or get a "free angry" whenever that
person pushes you too far (or pushes you at all)? Do you gain
the controller's approval, maintain your relationship, have a
handy excuse not to focus on your own weaknesses?

On one side of a sheet of paper, list everything you gain,
don't lose, or don't have to change by reacting to controlling
people the way you typically do. On the other side of the page,
list the consequences you suffer, the price you pay for continuing to do things as you've always done them. (For example: How
stressful is your life? What sort of physical toll has being stuck
in a control trap taken on you?)

Once you have listed the benefits and costs of your current

behavior patterns, assign each a numerical weight. Use numbers between 1 and 10 (1 = the least; 10 = the most) to indicate how much satisfaction each of your payoffs provides and how much distress each consequence causes. Tally the weights in each column and compare totals. If the costs outweigh the benefits, then it may be time to start thinking about making a change.

PART TWO

TAKING BACK THE POWER

CHAPTER
5

TAKING BACK THE POWER
THE AIKIDO ALTERNATIVE

You'll remember Emma, who constantly worried that something would go wrong with her daughter's upcoming wedding, and became a control freak to make certain nothing did. Here is how one of their typical phone conversations sounded. In this instance, Emma wanted Lisa to arrange for backup entertainment for the reception, in case the band currently under contract canceled out or didn't show up.

EMMA: . . . so as soon as the agency opens, call to arrange a backup musical group. And make sure you get a *good* one.

LISA: Mom, I don't really think that's necessary. The group we have will be able to make it. I've checked with—

EMMA: Oh, God, here we go again! Why can't you do the simplest thing I ask? How can you be so insensitive after all the time—and let's be honest, all the money —I've put into this. And think of Dad. If you cared the least bit for *his* happiness, you'd—

LISA: (Sounding angry) Mom, Dad doesn't care! He doesn't even like music! He'll—

EMMA: Oh, Lisa, how can you raise your voice to me after everything I've done. It isn't like this is *my* wedding I'm spending half my life on . . .

Lisa absolutely dreaded these calls. She knew her mother well, and could predict how the phone conversation would go. Emma would continue to make her demands, liberally salting them with emotionally exploitative hooks and triggers. Lisa would get angrier and angrier, until she finally exploded or hung up. Later, consumed with guilt, she would call back and wind up agreeing to her mother's requests—hating herself all the while for being so weak.

But let's say that Lisa (having read this book) decides to try something different. She doesn't know exactly what else to do, but she's had it with the "fight back/feel guilty/give in" pattern. Rather than simply trying harder, she's ready to try something else. What else can she try? What other alternatives are available to her?

Five Alternatives

There are at least five general types of responses you can make to someone who is trying to control you. Two of these, *giving in* and *fighting back*, have been covered at some length in Chapter 4. Most accommodators either give in or fight back—or, like Lisa, use a combination of these two options. They do so automatically, often without realizing other alternatives are available, and the consequences generally aren't very pleasant.

The other three options available to you are *disconnecting*, *leveling*, and what we call the *aikido alternative*, which parallels the martial art of the same name. Although we'll focus most of our attention in this chapter on aikido, there are situations in which one of the other four possibilities might work best. There are times to level with control freaks, and times to avoid dealing with them if you possibly can. There are times to give in to their demands (at least temporarily), and there are even times to go head-to-head with them and fight it out.

Giving In and Fighting Back

While the control freak is making his move, emotions and tensions can be high, and many people see fighting or folding as the only things they can do. They respond automatically. But rather than being only knee-jerk reactions, giving in and fighting back also can be used as conscious, *strategic* choices.

Choosing to Give In   Under some circumstances, allowing yourself to be controlled may be the only practical option available to you. In others, giving isn't just your "least bad" choice— it is absolutely the best way to get where you want to go. Still, there are people who never give in if they can help it. They equate giving in with losing, they think it makes them look weak, or they simply fight to the death as a matter of principle. From a strategic point of view, this is unfortunate: when the situation calls for giving in, they are stuck. If you find yourself in a position where giving in seems like your best, only, or most practical choice, then *make that choice.*

Try not to resent it, carry anger around about it, or beat yourself up because you "lost." You *didn't* lose; you chose the best option available to you under the circumstances. For more on choosing to give in, see *Writing It into Your Job Description* in Chapter 9.

103

TIMES TO CONSIDER GIVING IN

- When doing anything else would be dangerous. Whenever the consequences of *not* giving in could seriously harm you, your family, your career or something else important to you, don't feel bad about choosing to throw in the towel and living to fight another day.

- When you want to establish a give-and-take relationship: Even when dealing with a control freak, it is reasonable to compromise. The other person eventually may begin to realize you're not simply trying to beat her in every hand, and become a bit more flexible herself.

- When giving in is part of your game plan. It makes sense to give in on something relatively unimportant in a way that will increase your bargaining power with a more important issue at a future date.

- When you're wrong. The person who fesses up when he's wrong gains respect (usually) and increases the chances that others may believe him when he's right.

- When you're going to lose anyway. Find a way to give in that will lose you as little as possible and may gain you something back in the process. Giving in early, giving in graciously or initiating the yielding process may have some strategic value.

Fighting It Out As used here, "fighting" means meeting force with force—when the control freak pushes, you push back. When the other person argues his point, you respond by arguing yours with equal or even greater force. We need to define our terms here, because most people also think of martial artists such as aikido or judo players as "fighters." While it is true that some martial arts (e.g., karate) emphasize meeting force with force, others do not. Arts such as judo and aikido operate on a very different principle, which involves *using* the strength of the opponent's attack rather than trying to overcome it. The core of this approach is sometimes called "alignment," and will be covered in detail later in the book.

My personal view is that there are usually better alternatives available than fighting. But not always. The standup comic deals with audience hecklers by heckling right back. An executive out-argues an associate who uses rational tactics to take control. An overworked teacher tells the class cut-up to sit down and get to work or take a two-hour detention. In each of these cases, there may have been a more gentle, more elegant alternative available. But it would have taken more time and effort, and might not have worked as well. For all practical purposes, fighting back was fine.

Just be sure *you* are choosing the fight—don't let the fight choose you. And be sure that you fight strategically—that is, fight in a way that the control freak won't be able to use against you down the road. Fighting at the wrong time, in the wrong place or with the wrong weapons can be disastrous.

TIMES TO CONSIDER FIGHTING BACK

- When fighting is the most effective or easiest solution. There may be more gentle, more elegant alternatives available, but it would have taken more time and effort and might not have worked as well.

- When a fight seems to be "needed." A fair fight can clear the air and promote intimacy: fights really can bring people closer together. Sometimes little frustrations build up over time, and fighting provides a release. You both yell a little, stomp around, act righteous— then make up.

- When fighting is what you want, and you are willing to take the consequences. Sometimes it just feels good to fight back, stand toe to toe, put it on the line.

Disconnecting

Nowhere is it written that when a controller makes his move, you have to participate in the process. Sometimes getting out of the situation—without doing anything about the control move one way or the other—is the best possible course of action. It isn't always possible to avoid dealing with a control freak, but when you can choose to avoid it, do so. Sometimes, of course, circumstances force you to interact. Other times you want to interact, because you believe the potential payoff is worth the attendant risks, hassles and discomfort. But when circumstances permit, disconnecting in some way may be the best choice you can make.

105

Basically, there are three ways to disconnect from a control freak. You can *leave*, either physically or psychologically (or force the controller to leave). You can *avoid*, by anticipating a control move and then eluding it in some way. Or you can *ignore* the control move by recognizing it and then choosing not to respond.

Lisa, of course, could disconnect literally—by hanging up the phone. (Lisa often did hang up, but not before making trouble for herself.) Or she could inform her mother (firmly, but pleasantly and without anger) that she would end the conversation unless the subject of backup entertainment was tabled. She might avoid similar early-morning conversations by getting an answering machine that would allow her to screen incoming calls, and give her the option to return her mother's calls at a time when she was most ready to deal with Emma. She might simply ignore what her mother was saying, but without hanging up. Or she might mislead her mother, agreeing to call the backup band and then simply not doing so until the spirit moved her.

For a more comprehensive list of ways to disconnect, see the accompanying box.

WAYS TO DISCONNECT FROM A CONTROL FREAK

- Leave the scene. Walk away, end a telephone conversation, excuse yourself to go to the rest room or, on a larger scale, get a new job or get out of a bad marriage.

- Spend less time with people who get to you. You don't have to call your control-freak mother *every* day, have lunch with your control-freak friend whenever she asks, or continue to ride to work with a colleague who spends the entire drive telling you how to do your job.

- Overlook things that may be irritating but don't really hurt you.

- Choose not to chase disconnectors—allow them to sulk or pout without repeatedly asking them what's wrong or doing things you think will make them feel better.

- Ignore insults, sarcastic comments, and other material intended to get a rise out of you.

- Thank donors for unsolicited advice but disregard their suggestions unless they offer you an alternative you'd like to pursue.

- Don't ask for a control freak's permission unless it's absolutely necessary. You'll find that it is less of a hassle to ask for forgiveness after the fact than to get controlling people to agree with you or approve your plans ahead of time.

- Stop trying to get other people to agree with you unless you absolutely need that agreement. Winning control freaks over to your point of view is not always a prerequisite for getting the job done.

Some of these ideas may rub you the wrong way. They're not all strictly honest, and they're not all particularly nice. Please understand: ignoring, misleading, or hanging up on your spouses, parents, or work associates is generally not the best way to proceed. These tactics are for use with people who are trying to coerce or manipulate you into doing or thinking or feeling what *they* want you to. They are trying to control you, and, as an alternative to giving in or fighting back, you have the unimpeachable right to cut the lines of communication that would allow them to do so. How radical your withdrawal needs to be depends on the circumstances, as well as on how far you personally are willing to go.

There may be negative consequences to some forms of disconnection. Several of the tactics listed here definitely fall into the "last resort" category. But they work, and, until you can come up with a better alternative, they may be your best bet.

Leveling

Leveling means being honest, telling the controller what you want or don't want from him, what you think about the outcome he's trying to achieve, how you feel about his behavior and what you are willing or unwilling to do. Sometimes a leveler may sound angry or frustrated, but in general, leveling is a "rational" tactic. That is, the purpose of leveling is to convey information to the controller, rather than evaluate or criticize his behavior, punish him, or change him in any way (see box). Of course, if you "level" with the controller in an angry, disparaging tone, while letting him know in no uncertain terms where he can put his demands, you aren't really leveling. You may be conveying information, but you are also fighting back.

WAYS TO LEVEL WITH A CONTROL FREAK

- Ask for five minutes of time with your controller and set out one or two simple ways you would like to change your relationship. Ask him or her to wait before responding.

- Clearly let the controller know what you find absolutely unacceptable.

- Tell the controller how you feel about the way he or she has been treating you.

- Clearly tell your controller what you *like* about his or her behavior, your relationship, or changes you see happening.

- If you can't confront the controller in person, write a short letter describing your thoughts and feelings.

- Ask your boss/spouse/friend for a weekly ten-minute session to clear the air. Each person gets five minutes to share gripes. Don't respond to each other, just listen.

- If you can't confront your controller, level with yourself first. Write out a list of what's bugging you and what you would like to do about it. Next time you interact with your control freak, keep those points in mind.

108

If Lisa decided to level with her mother, she might *state her position* regarding Emma's demands and accusations and *set some limits* regarding what she, Lisa, might be willing to do, and under what circumstances. A portion of their conversation might go something like this:

LISA: (Responding to Emma's last comment, (page 101) Look, Mom, I don't mean to shout at you. But I'm feeling a little frustrated. With everything else I have to do, arranging a backup band just isn't on the top of my priority list. There are so many things on my mind—

EMMA: Of course there are, there always are. You've been that way your whole life, always thinking of yourself. Well, if it weren't for me, young lady, you wouldn't even be having a wedding.

LISA: Mom, I'm getting a little upset. I do appreciate what you've done, and I think it's unfair for you to imply that I don't. Anyway, I have to go in a couple of minutes—can we talk about something else?

EMMA: Sure, go ahead and change the subject! How do you think I'm going to feel when all my friends come to the reception and there's no entertainment because you didn't care enough to make one phone call?

LISA: I really don't want to discuss the wedding, Mom. If you insist on bringing it up, I'm going to say "goodbye" now.

The Value of Leveling Leveling is simple, straightforward and honest. When it works, it is often the most effective way to proceed. Both parties can get their issues on the table and begin working them out. In addition, leveling is easy to learn. Basically, the idea is to use short, simple sentences and repeat yourself a lot, until the controller begins to hear what you are saying. Also, remember to mention positive feelings and behaviors you like as well as negative feelings and behaviors you don't like. The KISS ("Keep It Short and Simple") model applies to leveling. In many control situations, this is the first alternative you should try.

Problems with Leveling Leveling is difficult to do effectively when you are upset. In her current state of mind, Lisa would have found it virtually impossible to have held that conversation according to our script. Sooner or later, her mother's constant criticisms and put-downs would strike a nerve; Lisa would lose control, get angry, and begin to respond in kind.

Even when you are able to level, the sad fact is that honesty and direct, forthright communication don't always work particularly well in the real world. For one thing, telling a control freak what you think and feel can make you vulnerable to later attack —sometime down the road you may well hear your own words coming back at you. If she wanted to, Emma could use some of the information Lisa "shared" with her to make her daughter look insensitive, uncaring or (especially if the original band doesn't show up) incredibly naive.

More important, honesty isn't always the gift it is sometimes made out to be in the self-help literature. Some forms of leveling can be cruel and hurtful. In the 1960s and early '70s, when confrontation-oriented encounter groups were so popular, a tremendous amount of pain was inflicted on innocent parents, spouses and lovers in the name of "honesty." It is the rare friendship, and the even rarer marriage, that can stand up to total honesty. White lies, politeness rituals, selective omissions and similar tactics are absolutely vital to the survival of most relationships—whether we want to admit it or not.

Even when not actively destructive, the receiver sometimes experiences direct honesty as heavy-handed, just a little rude. As a matter of fact, North America is one of the few places in the world where direct, assertive communication is highly valued. Most cultures favor a more indirect style. For example, it would be unacceptable for a traditional Japanese woman to deal with her mother as Lisa dealt with Emma in the last script, no matter what the circumstances. Many of you may have found that excerpt a bit distasteful as well.

Leveling *is* a valuable alternative; however, it often works best when used in combination with an approach that can leave the other person feeling appreciated and understood as well as confronted and informed. This brings us to my favorite set of tactics: the "aikido alternative."

The Aikido Alternative

Think about being behind the wheel of your car when it hits a patch of ice and starts to skid. The car veers to the right and your immediate inclination is to turn the steering wheel to the left. However, you will actually regain control of the car more quickly if you steer *into* the skid, turning the wheel in the direction the car is already sliding. Seems crazy (at least to those of us who aren't used to driving on icy roads), but it works. As a matter of fact, if you steer in the opposite direction trying to keep your car out of the ditch, you may well wind up in a spinning car, and eventually in the very ditch you were trying to avoid.

The same principle applies to your conflicts and confrontations with control freaks. When someone is trying his best to control you and you don't want to be controlled, it's natural to fight back, matching his attack with an equally powerful defense. But if you do that, all you wind up with is a power struggle. If the control freak is stronger than you are, or is better at attacking than you are at defending or counterattacking, you may have a problem.

Of course, as you know by now, there is another option available. The aikido alternative would have you deal with that control freak the same way you dealt with your skidding car. Rather than immediately trying to stop the attack, you move *with* the other person's energy for a while. This technique is called *alignment,* and is central to the practice of aikido. The idea is that once you're in alignment with the controller's energy, you may be able to begin to influence it, possibly redirecting it, or neutralizing it in some way—just as you were able to regain control of your car.

Aikido is really a kind of applied systems theory. Its students see their essential purpose as attaining and maintaining a condition of harmony, within themselves and between themselves and the environment. When attacked, they don't try to beat the attacker; technically, they don't even fight back. Rather, they see an attacker as someone who is not *balanced* (people who attack other people are out of balance by definition), and therefore in need of assistance. They simply provide the assistance needed, in a way that neutralizes the attack and does as little harm as possible to everyone involved, the attacker included.

(Now, if you asked him, the attacker might not *agree* he'd been assisted. Generally, attackers tend not to see martial artists as assisting them. But from the aikido player's perspective, he did not beat an opponent or win a fight, because there was no fight. There was only an intervention, a realignment and a restoration of harmony.)

111

The basic principles underlying the practice of aikido apply to all kinds of human interaction, and many of the movements have non-physical analogues *which can be used to neutralize verbal assault and other control tactics.* In addition, the self-control exercises aikido players use to maintain their own harmony and balance in the face of attack and possible injury can be of great value to people who must deal with control freaks on a daily basis and risk emotional, psychological, or even physical injury in the process.

FOUR BASIC AIKIDO SKILLS

- *Centering* is the ability to relax, breathe and stay physically and emotionally balanced no matter what else may be going on.

- *Paying Attention* simply means carefully observing what is going on around you—no matter what might be going on around you.

- *Aligning* means to move with, rather than fight against or give in to, an opponent's energy. Roughly analogous communication skills might be empathizing and establishing rapport. Good alignment is usually necessary before you can begin to redirect.

> • *Redirecting* is an extension of alignment, and means moving or changing the attacking energy in some way, eventually neutralizing it or even finding a way to put it to positive use.

Aikido and Control Freaks   Essentially, the aikido alternative involves recognizing and understanding other people's needs or motives and *helping them meet at least some of those needs,* so that they will not feel compelled to continue to control you or give you a hard time. For instance, Janet arrives home from work and says "Hi" to her husband, John. John turns around and just about bites her head off. Clearly he is not in the best of moods; he seems mad at the world in general and at Janet in particular.

If Janet decided to use the aikido alternative, she would ask herself, "Okay, what does John need to get from me that might help him be a little more pleasant to be around?" Janet may or may not have an answer to that question. If she doesn't, she'll try to find out—she might try a few things, she might ask John directly, or she might lie low for a while and observe. Then, to the extent that it doesn't interfere too much with her *own* needs and priorities, she'll try to help John reduce the needs that are making him such an ogre.

While that may sound like the same old self-sacrificing, people-pleasing approach that got you in trouble in the first place and that women in particular are programmed to use, it is not. Janet is not expected to change her most important priorities. Rather, she will look for compromises and win-win solutions that will meet some of John's needs and also take care of some of her own.

In general, the aikido alternative offers a collaborative way to work with the control freak which, at least initially, does not require that person's cooperation (a major limitation in many approaches to conflict resolution.) You begin the process simply by paying close attention to every nuance of the other person's behavior, collecting as much data as possible from the signals he transmits before and during his control move. Although your past experience with the control freak may give you a tentative idea of how he will behave under certain conditions, prior knowledge is not a substitute for paying attention. Your prediction may turn out to be accurate, but by observing and analyzing the controller's actual behavior, you will also be prepared to deal with what happens if your prediction is wrong.

When you are ready to make your first move, it will be one that aligns with the controller. You do this by going along with selected elements of the other person's communication style, matching the rhythm or cadence of his speech, or his tone of voice, using similar jargon, acknowledging his feelings, summarizing what you've heard or mirroring certain aspects of his body language. If possible, you agree with at least some of the points the controller is making.

By aligning yourself with the other person's patterns rather than using your own automatic style, you are sending the message, "I'm trying to understand. I'm trying to speak the same language you are. I'm interested in what is important to *you.*" That sets the stage for the two of you to become collaborators rather than adversaries. It is also quite disarming for control freaks, who don't expect you to blend and move *with* them. The interaction is not proceeding in the way they planned or pictured it in their mind's eye, and when that dawns on them, they will pause to collect their thoughts and reassess their strategy— giving you an opportunity to step in and redirect the interaction.

113

Practical Applications

If you don't quite get how the aikido alternative works as yet, that's okay. This was just a brief overview of a complex process that will be explained in more detail as you learn the skills you'll need to use it. It will become clearer as you go along. The following examples, drawn from anecdotes that appeared earlier in this book, may help you visualize the aikido alternative in action.

Lisa and Emma

Using the aikido alternative, Lisa might align with Emma by sympathizing with her, perhaps saying, "You *have* done an enormous amount of work on our wedding and Jeff and I haven't let you know how much we appreciate it."

Although such a response would certainly surprise Emma, it probably wouldn't stop her dead in her tracks. She'd probably complain for a while longer and get a few more of her disaster fantasies out into the open. Lisa would continue to go along with her mother.

"I never realized so many things could go wrong," she might say. Or, "I'd never be able to keep track of all those details by myself." Such responses would fulfill Emma's need to be heard, reward her for her efforts, and reassure her that her daughter is on her side.

With her needs satisfied, Emma might begin to calm down and Lisa, who would be paying careful attention, would recognize that. She would begin to redirect. "I can really appreciate what you're going through because that's exactly what's happening to me today," she might say. "In fact, as soon as I get off the phone, I won't have another free minute until at least midnight. The way I see it, if arrangements must be made for a backup band today, I'm going to need you to handle it for me. But if it could wait until tomorrow or the next day, I'd be glad to do it."

No longer in a panic, Emma might go along with one of those options. The detail would be handled—fulfilling Emma's need—and Lisa would not have to drop everything to handle it immediately. Both would benefit—with practically no cost to either of them.

Alan and Kim

Remember Kim and Alan's conflict over the movie they saw on Kim's birthday? The entire confrontation might have been avoided if Kim had known about the aikido alternative. She would have been paying close attention when Alan sought her opinion on the movie and she would have recognized that his "Didn't you love it?" question was not really a question at all but a request for her to agree with him. Because loving or not loving the movie wasn't a life or death issue but not being nagged or put down by Alan *was* quite important to her, giving in might have been Kim's best bet and she could have chosen to tell Alan that she agreed with him—even though she did not.

Once she missed her cue, Kim still could have salvaged the situation with the aikido alternative. Using the same intensity and inflections as Alan used when he said, "I can't *believe* you didn't like it!" she might have responded to his minilecture by saying, "You *really* did your homework! I can't *believe* how much you know about this movie! Tell me what *else* you've heard about it!" Since Alan was going to tell her anyway, Kim would most definitely be moving in the direction he was going—but she wouldn't be feeling intimidated by him. Like Lisa, she could continue to align with Alan until his need to prove his intelligence, sophistication and superiority was satisfied and he wound down. Or she could have simultaneously redirected him by asking him questions that kept the focus off her ("And what did the *Times* critic say?" or "Did you feel that way about the other films so and so directed?"). Either way, as soon as Kim noticed that Alan was stating his case less forcefully, she could toss in one last compliment: "As always you amaze me. I'm absolutely floored by how much you know about movie making," and then change the subject.

Alan would have had the opportunity to boost his ego by expounding on a topic he considered his specialty—which was the payoff he was after—and Kim would have prevented Alan from browbeating her or backing her into a corner—which was the payoff she was after. Although Kim still would have to listen to Alan go on about the movie, she would never give up control of her own thoughts, feelings and actions and wouldn't feel nearly so anxious or upset when the interaction was over. Clearly, the benefits would have outweighed the costs.

115

Beverly and Ellen

If Beverly had employed the aikido alternative when Ellen delivered her kind gesture/barbed comment double message, their interaction might have gone this way:

Beverly acknowledges the positive side of the message: "What a lovely gift. Thank you for letting me know how much our friendship means to you."

Then she aligns with the negative side by asking, "How can I show you that our friendship is important to me too?"

Like Alan, Ellen is more than happy to provide Beverly with the information she requested. Beverly listens and continues going along with Ellen, sometimes paraphrasing exactly what she hears and sometimes subtly revising Ellen's thoughts.

For instance, Ellen says, "If we go someplace together you *should* stay with me instead of flitting around to socialize with people I don't know as well as you do." Beverly replies, "You *wish* I wouldn't spend so much time talking to other people when we're out together." Ellen feels that she is getting through to Beverly. Beverly knows that she isn't caving in. Both women are winning.

When Ellen runs out of directives, Beverly summarizes and opens negotiations, letting Ellen know that she feels comfortable with some items on Ellen's list, but thinks that others would be tough to do, especially under certain circumstances.

Unfortunately, Ellen is stuck in control mode and proceeds to tell Beverly exactly how to do what she wants. Beverly aligns again. "You would do it that way," she says. "I've always marveled at your ability to handle a dozen things at once." Ellen replies, "You could too if only you would . . ." And so it goes until Beverly says, "I'll have to try that one of these days, but for now I can only handle these three things. Could we see how that works out and worry about the other things later?"

Ellen grudgingly agrees and sulks for an hour or so. By the following morning, she has a whole new list of instructions for Beverly and they start their discussion all over again.

There are no guarantees. Because Ellen would not let go until she got everything she wanted, there was really no effective way to resolve the conflict. However, rather than automatically caving in, Beverly remained in control of her own responses, neither trying to please Ellen in advance nor berating herself after their interaction ended. She was still better off than she had been before.

116

Final Thoughts

In the next three chapters, you will explore practical ways to learn and use the aikido alternative. Remember, this is not the only way—and is sometimes not even the best way—to deal with controlling people. But if you try it, I think you'll find it a useful alternative. If the suggestions don't work, you can try something else or go back to your old methods.

But don't give up too quickly. Controllers operate out of habit; their behavior is part of a long-standing pattern and using a new response once or twice won't stop it. The controlling people in your life will not become pussycats just because you are reacting to them differently than you have in the past. They won't be taken down easily and they are quite likely to switch frequencies, trading one tactic for another.

TAKING BACK THE POWER

The authoritarian bully may begin acting like a pouting child, and the fragile manipulator may turn into a tantrum-throwing assailant. Some controllers will see even tiny steps toward collaboration as attempts to dominate them and will haul out their entire arsenal. Be prepared for resistance.

Also take heart. If you make their controlling behavior ineffective often enough, eventually most control freaks will back off. And even if they don't, you'll still be able to respond in a way that serves you. You'll fulfill at least some of your needs, and you'll no longer lose control of your own thoughts, feelings or actions.

CHAPTER
6

CENTERING
PATHWAYS TO PERSONAL POWER

"WITH SMALL FLAGS WAVING AND TINY BLASTS OF TINY TRUMPETS, WE HAS
MET THE ENEMY—AND IT IS US."

—WALT KELLEY, *Pogo*

This chapter will help you meet and overcome "the enemy who is you." Control freaks wouldn't have nearly so easy a time driving us bonkers if we didn't help them out. Not that we necessarily *intend* to help them, mind you. But the array of fears, doubts, stored resentments, self-defeating behaviors, conflicts, self-esteem problems, and unfulfilled needs we carry around with us from day to day *and don't do anything about* make us easy targets. Sometimes the controller doesn't even have to aim very carefully.

Let's return to our friend Lisa. In the last chapter you saw how she behaved during a phone conversation with Emma. Here is a glimpse of the internal reactions that accompanied her behavior.

When Lisa heard her mother's voice, her shoulder muscles began to tighten. Emma's voice tone and manner clearly signaled she was going to begin making demands. Lisa's teeth clenched, her breathing became rapid and shallow, adrenaline began to pump into her system. All she could think was, "I hate this, she has no right to treat me this way." But simultaneously, another little voice whispered, "But she's your mother. . . ."

Lisa believed that the best way to deal with Emma was to remain a calm, rational adult. But that was easier said than done. Her mother's voice and manner made Lisa feel small and incompetent, like a weak and helpless child. She abhorred feeling that way.

Lisa felt trapped by the sound of Emma's voice. She became acutely aware of every nuance, every inflection, every change in tone—yet at the same time she could barely understand the words Emma was saying. She couldn't seem to focus, and could no longer think of what she wanted to say. She felt a little dizzy, and found it hard to concentrate. Helpless rage began to engulf her, quickly dissolving her recent resolve to stay in control the next time Emma called.

Finally, the dam broke: Lisa exploded into an angry tirade and slammed down the receiver. Then, almost as the phone hit the cradle, the guilt feelings, the self-recriminations, and the doubts ("Maybe I can't really make it on my own; I shouldn't have treated her that way") began to grow. She spent a terrible half hour, then picked up the phone and began to dial.

Fight-or-Flight

119

Lisa experienced a complex variation of what physiologists have long called the "fight-or-flight" reaction. Fight-or-flight is an autonomic survival response—when the body senses danger, it prepares itself in various ways for intense activity and the need for extra energy. Adrenaline is pumped into the bloodstream, blood (and therefore oxygen and nutrients) is directed away from the glands and into the muscles, breathing becomes more rapid, glandular secretion decreases (leading to a dry mouth and other common signs of anxiety), and the individual generally feels an increase in nervous tension.

It is easy to see why our primitive ancestors needed a fight-or-flight response. The world back then was a dangerous place, and when danger threatened, Ooga the cavewoman didn't have the time (or the brain cells) to sit down and figure out what to do. If a cave bear or pterodactyl appeared, Ooga had to get moving *now!*

Well, the world is still a dangerous place, but these days many of the dangers are different and require different responses. When falling money markets threaten the new company bond issue, or when the phone rings and it's Emma, a relaxed manner and some cool, strategic thinking are called for.

Unfortunately, what comes up is fight-or-flight, accompanied (now that we have the brain cells) by catastrophic fantasies, negative self-talk, irrational beliefs, low self-esteem and other pieces of programmed psychological flotsam that only serve to make matters worse. The nervous energy that would have helped us fight the pterodactyl has nowhere to go, and begins to short-circuit. The problem is, our bodies still believe in pterodactyls, but all the pterodactyls are gone. Only Emma is left, and dealing with Emma requires a new set of responses.

Inner Harmony

It isn't just that our antiquated survival mechanisms and strategies can't handle the challenges of modern living. They also keep us from learning and using more effective methods. The aikido master may look graceful and almost unconcerned as he aligns with and then redirects an attack. But he didn't come by it easily. Serious aikido students spend several hours per week practicing the meditation and visualization exercises that will allow them to maintain a state of inner harmony no matter what else may be going on around them.

The same is true for Lisa. No matter how many communication courses she takes, no matter how many self-help books she reads, Lisa's ability to deal with her mother will not change much until she finds a way to modify her automatic programming.

But when she learns to stay *centered* (relaxed, alert, and emotionally balanced) during one of Emma's calls, the game will change dramatically. Not only will Lisa suffer less, she also will regain the ability to use with Emma the interpersonal skills and self-confidence that helped her become a successful and respected businesswoman. While she still may not be able to satisfy Emma in a way that also works for her, she'll at least be able to give it her best shot.

Understanding Your Automatic Reactions

The first step in learning to deal with automatic reactions is to find out exactly what they are. First, we'll take a more systematic look at the ways in which Lisa reacted to her mother's call.

120

Then you'll have a chance to explore some of your own reactions to the control freaks in your lives.

Reaction Categories

Automatic reactions can be broken down in any number of ways. We'll use five categories, or modes: *behaviors, feelings, sensations, imagery,* and *thoughts,* which roughly correspond to the five personal "modalities" used by Dr. Arnold A. Lazarus of Rutgers University. Dr. Lazarus developed a very powerful and flexible approach to clinical treatment he calls "multimodal therapy." His ideas and teachings have had a great impact on me, and many of them are reflected in the pages of this book.

Behaviors   Problem behaviors that are commonly triggered by control freaks include blushing, stuttering, disrupted breathing, crying, inability to maintain eye contact, defensiveness, automatic apologizing, physical tension and so on.

121

When Lisa heard her mother's voice, the muscles in her chest and shoulders tensed. Her breathing faltered, then became rapid and shallow. She clenched her teeth. Later in the conversation she shouted at her mother and then hung up.

Feelings   Lisa felt angry and apprehensive during her phone conversation. Later in the process, she felt guilty and ashamed both for blowing up at Emma, and for losing control of herself *again.* She also reported feeling "small and weak, like a helpless child."

Sensations   Lisa reported feeling hypersensitive to Emma's tone of voice, but unable to hear many of Emma's words. She felt flushed and somewhat "disconnected." In general, Lisa reported feeling just a little "unreal" during these conversations— as if her body were going through the motions, and she was just along for the ride.

Imagery   Lisa didn't report much in the way of visual imagery, although many trainees do. One man, who feared rejection from authority figures, cold-called the CEO of a small company to introduce a new service. As he described it, "I heard the executive's voice and suddenly found myself picturing an austere, gray-haired businessman looking contemptuously at me, then turning away. . . . The knot in my stomach tightened and I began to feel like an inadequate child."

Thoughts This category includes self-talk, values, "shoulds" and so on. General self-image problems belong here, as do issues relating to inner conflict. Lisa's self-talk included such phrases as "I hate this!" and "But, she's your mother." In addition, Lisa believed she should be able to deal calmly with Emma's demands and was critical of herself because she couldn't.

Assessing Your Reactions

Now it is your turn. Two methods have been developed which may help you become aware of how you react under pressure. One of these requires nothing more than pencil and paper. The next time you have a difficult encounter, pay careful attention to your reactions. Afterward, describe them in terms of Lozarus' 5 modalities (as Lisa's reactions were described earlier). If you have a friend who would like to get involved, ask him or her to interview you. Your friend may be able to help you recall portions of the experience that you would have been unable to remember on your own.

Sometimes it is useful to have a more structured tool available. The Confrontation Questionnaire provides that structure.

CONFRONTATION QUESTIONNAIRE

Think of a time in the recent past when you had to deal with a controlling person and you did not do as well as you would have liked.

Close your eyes for a moment and recall the situation as best you can. Visualize the person's face, remember the sound of his/her voice. Recall what he or she said, how s/he acted. Remember how you felt as you dealt with this person's attempt to control you. How did you react?

The following questionnaire will help you assess what may have gone wrong and what you can do to improve things for next time. Answer each item as it pertains to the interaction you just thought about. Please respond to each item —if you can't remember how you felt or acted regarding a particular question, make your best guess.

CENTERING

		Not Accurate	Somewhat Accurate	Very Accurate		

PART A:
BEFORE THE
INTERACTION*

1.	I worried about how I would perform.	1	2	3	4	5
2.	I worried about what the controller might say to me.	1	2	3	4	5
3.	I felt tense and anxious.	1	2	3	4	5
4.	I pictured the controller intimidating, attacking or rejecting me.	1	2	3	4	5
5.	I tried not to think about it.	1	2	3	4	5
6.	I was pretty sure I wouldn't do a very good job.	1	2	3	4	5
7.	I felt disoriented, slightly dizzy, or couldn't concentrate.	1	2	3	4	5
8.	I imagined failing or making a fool of myself.	1	2	3	4	5
9.	I noticed my breathing was more rapid and shallow than normal.	1	2	3	4	5
10.	I felt angry at the controller.	1	2	3	4	5

123

*If you didn't know the interaction was coming, make your best guess, based on past experience, about how you would have thought and felt if you *had* known.

		Not Accurate		Somewhat Accurate		Very Accurate

PART B: DURING THE INTERACTION

11.	I went blank.	1	2	3	4	5
12.	I responded without thinking.	1	2	3	4	5
13.	I felt angry.	1	2	3	4	5
14.	I remembered the last time I dealt with this (or a similar) person.	1	2	3	4	5
15.	I thought s/he was probably right and I was wrong.	1	2	3	4	5
16.	I felt afraid.	1	2	3	4	5
17.	I felt shaky.	1	2	3	4	5
18.	I couldn't think of anything to say.	1	2	3	4	5
19.	I imagined other people watching me fail or make a fool of myself.	1	2	3	4	5
20.	I found myself saying things I knew I would regret later.	1	2	3	4	5
21.	Portions of my body (shoulders, stomach, neck, etc.) became tense.	1	2	3	4	5
22.	I was afraid my voice would quiver or break.	1	2	3	4	5
23.	I saw myself as small or weak in relation to the controller.	1	2	3	4	5

		Not Accurate		Somewhat Accurate	Very Accurate	
24.	I lost my temper, or was afraid I might lose my temper.	1	2	3	4	5
25.	I cried, or was afraid I might cry.	1	2	3	4	5
26.	I pictured myself doing something foolish or inappropriate.	1	2	3	4	5
27.	I was not firm or assertive enough.	1	2	3	4	5
28.	I couldn't seem to think quickly enough.	1	2	3	4	5
29.	At times I held my breath.	1	2	3	4	5
30.	I noticed a flushed or tingling feeling (or similar sensations).	1	2	3	4	5

PART C: AFTER THE INTERACTION

31.	I felt ashamed of my performance.	1	2	3	4	5
32.	I couldn't get the controller's face out of my mind.	1	2	3	4	5
33.	I felt disconnected from the experience, almost as if it hadn't really happened.	1	2	3	4	5
34.	I remained agitated for at least fifteen minutes.	1	2	3	4	5

	Not Accurate		Somewhat Accurate		Very Accurate
35. I kept running the interaction over and over in my mind.	1	2	3	4	5
36. I couldn't relax.	1	2	3	4	5
37. I wanted to contact the controller and apologize.	1	2	3	4	5
38. I thought of things I wished I'd said during the interaction.	1	2	3	4	5
39. I couldn't remember much about the conversation.	1	2	3	4	5
40. I felt sure I'd done a bad job.	1	2	3	4	5

This questionnaire can be scored in various ways. The overall score reflects how *generally blocked* you felt with regard to this encounter. The situation score (totals for before, during, and after) will show you *when* your most serious problems occur. As before, an *average* score of above about "3" may indicate you have some work to do. And ratings on individual items will reflect specific reactions or barriers which you may then undertake to change. The most practical way to use the survey seems to be to focus on the individual items. Pay particular attention to the ones you marked "4" or "5". You'll see how they can be used in the next section.

Reprogramming Automatic Responses

There are a great number of exercises available to help you reduce the automatic reactions that showed up as significant problems on your questionnaire. This book could never present them all. Instead, here is a detailed description of how Lisa proceeded to recognize and attack reactions to her mother's demanding phone calls. Each of the specific exercises she used will be described quickly as well. Lisa's story will show you how a *modular* approach to reprogramming (see box) can be systematically applied. In addition, you'll get some ideas for structuring a similar program to help you deal with your own automatic reactions.

MODULAR REPROGRAMMING

Break down what you need to learn into small discrete steps (or "modules"). Practice the steps exhaustively one at a time. Then combine them into the change strategy. The larger strategy is then practiced as a whole. (See the sample reprogramming worksheet on page 129.)

The following analogy may help you understand how *modular reprogramming* works. Imagine your automatic reactions are like a huge, tangled net keeping you from reaching your goal. Some people run into the net and try to fight their way through it. Others steer clear of the net, and choose other goals which seem easier to reach. Still others sit around griping about how unfair it is that there's a net in the way.

The reprogrammer simply walks to the net and studies it for a while. Then she takes out her nail clippers and *cuts a single interlacing.* Of course, nothing much happens. She cuts a second cord, and then a third. Still, nothing seems to be happening, but in fact the structural integrity of the entire net is weakening. Eventually the reprogrammer will cut an interlacing, and a portion of the net will fall down. A few more cords, and other sections fall; soon she is free to walk easily toward her goal through the huge hole she's made in the net.

In modular reprogramming, each exercise is intended to clip one "interlacing." Don't look for immediate, dramatic changes in your ability to deal with control freaks. Do your homework, and let the net weaken. If you stick with it, the final results will be worth the wait.

Lisa's Story

Several months after the wedding ceremony, Lisa attended a seminar on dealing with difficult people, to see if she could sort out her relationship with Emma once and for all. Things had quieted down somewhat after the wedding, but there were still problems. Furthermore, Lisa and Jeff were now thinking of having a child. She didn't need much imagination to picture the field day Emma could have with her daughter's pregnancy, and then with the birth of *Emma's grandchild*. Lisa wanted to be prepared.

Lisa's General Goal

Summarizing her description of the outcome(s) she wished to achieve from her training, Lisa said, "I guess it boils down to three things. First, I want to be able to stay calm when Mom calls, not get my dander up no matter how nervous she gets and no matter what she says to me. Second, I want to be able to say no to her ridiculous demands without having to defend myself and then feel guilty afterward. And third, I'd like to do whatever I can to get Mom to back off a bit, be sensitive to my needs and fears as well as to her own." Notice that Lisa's objectives involve making changes in *her own* behavior and reactions ("I want to . . ."), rather than in Emma's ("I want Mom to . . .").

Lisa's Reprogramming Worksheet

Working from Lisa's written descriptions and questionnaire results, Lisa, with her friend and training partner, Tracy, to help her, produced a list of target reactions. They entered these in Column 1 of Lisa's reprogramming worksheet (see box). Column 2, a list of the techniques to be used for each reaction, was filled in as the seminar progressed.

LISA'S REPROGRAMMING WORKSHEET

Target Reactions	Technique
• Physical tension	Tension-release relaxation
• Rapid, shallow breathing when speaking to Emma	Abdominal breathing
• Holds breath when attacked	Stress-inoculation role-play. Breathing while dealing with verbal attack.
• Feelings of dizziness, floating, disconnection	Oak tree visualization
• Weak, powerless feeling	Power place visualization
• Feeling of being overwhelmed by Emma during phone conversation	Resource stacking visualization
• Self-doubts, esteem problems	Affirmations
• Dealing with Emma's anger	Stress-inoculation role-play—intensity-matching
• Dealing with Emma's guilt trips	Stress-inoculation role-play—deflecting emotional hooks
• General reactions to Emma's phone call and demands	Combined strategy (visualization) Combined strategy (role-play)

129

The exercises Lisa used come from a variety of sources. Some are *energy flow* drills derived from techniques aikido players use to help them stay centered and "grounded" under attack. Others are used in management training seminars, or in personal growth workshops. Let's join Lisa as she works through some of these reprogramming exercises.

Tension-Release Relaxation

Sitting in a comfortable chair, Lisa alternately tensed and released the muscles in her entire body. She took a deep breath, let some of it out, then tensed every major muscle group: her arms, legs, neck, face, stomach and so on. She also tensed her chest and diaphragm, squeezing the air in her lungs. As she did so, she focused all her attention on the sensations that accompanied the tension.

She held the tension for only a couple of seconds. Then she silently said the word "Relax," and let every muscle go. Her body sank in the chair and her breath came out in a *whoosh*. As she let go, she concentrated on the changes in sensation that came with the relaxation, and on exactly what she *did* when she let go. For about ten seconds she let her body relax even more, then silently said the word "Tense," and began another tension-release cycle. Four or five cycles and she was done for the session. Ideally, for the first few weeks, Lisa would perform three or four of these sessions a day.

130

Comment This exercise will help Lisa learn to relax more completely. In addition, she can use it whenever she feels tense, but especially before and/or during telephone conversations with her mother.

If you practice tension-release, don't forget to say "Tense" and "Relax" at the appropriate times. Eventually these words will induce a certain amount of tension or relaxation all by themselves, in much the same way that Pavlov's dogs learned to salivate to the sound of a bell. In programming vernacular, the words will become *triggers;* as you'll see, triggers can be very useful training aids.

Abdominal Breathing

Lisa either stood or sat with her hands on her abdomen. When the exercise began, she exhaled as much air as she could, and then inhaled by using her abdominal muscles to bring in air. As she inhaled, her muscles created a kind of a wave effect: she first expanded her abdomen, then her stomach, and finally her chest. She exhaled in reverse order, first from her chest, then her stomach, and finally her abdomen.

A common variation, which is similar to breath meditation, would have Lisa silently count her breaths, beginning with 1 and continuing to 10, saying the number on exhale. If she got distracted and lost her count, she would simply acknowledge the distraction and return her attention to her breathing, beginning again at one.

Comment This is a very simple exercise—please don't use that as a reason to underestimate its value. *Abdominal breathing* is considered "healthy" breathing by most experts. Air is forced more deeply into the lungs, which is both an efficient way to breathe and good for the lungs. Rapid, shallow breathing often is associated with anxiety, and is much less efficient from a physiological standpoint.

But whatever kind of breathing you do, *remember to breathe!* Many people hold their breath under stress. This is not a good idea for a variety of reasons: your energy will go down; you won't be able to think as well; and, other things equal, your physical tension level will increase.

Oak Tree Visualization

Lisa sat in the chair she normally used when on the phone with Emma. She put audiotaped instructions for the visualization exercise in her tape player, pushed the Play button, and closed her eyes (see box). As the exercise progressed, Lisa tried to "create the experience" of being a tree on as many sensory channels as possible. That is, she imagined she could *hear* the breeze sighing through her branches, the surf breaking on the beach far away. She tried to imagine what it would *feel* like to be an oak tree, focusing on feelings of solidness and calm, unshakable strength. She imagined her roots going deep into the ground, sucking up nourishment and energy the way a child drinks fruit juice through a straw. She remembered the *smell* and *taste* of a cool sea breeze.

131

OAK TREE VISUALIZATION—INSTRUCTIONS

(Tape these instructions, then use the tape as a guide until you know the exercise well enough to do it on your own.)

Sit or stand quietly, eyes closed, weight balanced, feet at shoulder width. Breathe regularly, maybe a little deeper and slower than normal. *(short pause)* Imagine that you are a large and venerable oak tree, hundreds of years old, standing on a grassy bluff overlooking the ocean. The air is warm, the sky blue; little white clouds sail quietly along. There is a pleasant breeze and the sound of the waves in the distance; somewhere a bird calls. Your roots are buried deep in the soil, and span out dozens of feet in all directions. You are deeply connected with the planet, so solid not even a bulldozer could push you over. You can visualize, almost feel, powerful, positive energy flowing up from the earth, through your roots, your trunk, your boughs. You can visualize your roots going down into the earth, hundreds of them, each so solidly gripping the earth and yet held by the earth, nurtured and protected, totally, serenely powerful and immovable. *(short pause)*

At the same time, your trunk goes up and up, branching and branching, each time into thinner, more delicate boughs, new growth of shoots and leaves, up into the blue sky. The wind blows through your branches, the willowy upper boughs move gently, the leaves are sensitive to the subtlest nuances in the breeze. Should a storm whip the wind to fury, your branches would bend and sway, flexibly rolling with the angry gale, still sensitive, still responding to each subtle difference, each tiny change in the wind. Yet your roots are so deep, so solid, that no storm could ever dislodge you from your knoll overlooking the sea. Solid, powerful, serene, yet sensitive, flexible, totally aware, from that solid, nurturing ground your branches and leaves ever reach out for more, beckoning for the sea, the sky . . . and the storm . . . to send you what they will . . . *(10–15 second pause).*

As you allow that image to fade, become aware of your arms, legs . . . the room around you . . . yet you can bring the feeling, the serenity, the power of the oak tree with you. Whatever you may see or hear may cause your branches to sway, but your roots will hold you firm. You can simply observe, *whatever* the experience may be, listen, watch, remember, but always as calm and serene as the venerable oak, grounded, at peace . . . *(Record 30 seconds of silence, followed by a click, tone or short, gentle verbal reminder that the exercise is over.)*

Most of all, Lisa *visualized* being connected and integrated with the world around her. She pictured energy flowing up from the ground through her trunk and branches, and out through her leaves. She pictured energy from the sun and wind entering her leaves, and flowing downward through her roots and into the soil. She imagined facing Emma, not alone, but rather as a small part of an incredibly powerful energy system against which Emma's petty demands and recriminations would be totally insignificant. When the taped instructions ended, Lisa gently brought the visualization to a close, and after affirming to herself that she could carry these images and feelings with her into the real world, she opened her eyes.

Comment   Lisa created a visual metaphor to help her access personal resources that already exist within her. Over the years, a great deal of research has been done on the use of imagery, and results consistently indicate its value and power. Unfortunately, daydreaming has taken on something of a negative connotation in Western cultures. In truth, properly structured and focused daydreams can be an important resource for people who want to overcome their old programming and learn new ways to react to old problems. Make sure you have some good ones in your own bag of tools. If the oak tree metaphor doesn't seem to be your cup of tea, then use images that are more to your liking.

133

Developing a "Power Place"

Lisa located in her own life a time and place when she felt confident and powerful. This turned out to be easy. Lisa was a successful designer; she felt proud of and confident in her abilities both as a businesswoman and as an artist. When she was in her Manhattan office, Lisa easily mustered just the kind of assurance and power she needed to be able to find when dealing with her mother.

She closed her eyes and imagined being at the office, sitting in her desk chair, about to close a major deal. She felt the rich leather of the chair, the solidness of her mahogany desk, the professional, efficient and *adult* feeling of the office. Most of all, she recalled the sense of herself in her business role: confident, in charge and able to handle anything that might come up.

Then she remembered instances when she'd dealt with difficult clients successfully. Lisa was particularly good at listening to their gripes and criticisms without taking any of it very personally. She could empathize with their concerns and sort out the valid ones from those that simply reflected the client's anxiety or ambivalence. She generally left her clients with the feeling that she sincerely cared about the project, and that she would take their concerns seriously. *At work,* Lisa was good at dealing with difficult people.

When she had a clear and complete image of her office and how she felt and functioned there, Lisa *brought the thumb and first two fingers of her right hand together and pressed firmly* for two or three seconds. Holding the image in her mind, she repeated this process four or five times. Then she gently bade goodbye to her office, her *power place,* and opened her eyes.

Comment   Clearly, Lisa would like to react to and deal with her mother as she does with her difficult clients. She can't do that now because the needs, memories, expectations and attitudes and self-image she associates with clients are very different from the ones linked to Emma.

The last part of the exercise, when Lisa put her thumb and fingers together, is intended to give her an additional method for accessing her power place when she needs to use it. She is establishing a "trigger," which she then associates with the appropriate image. As with the word "Relax," eventually she will find that touching her thumb and fingers together will help her recall —will help trigger—the feelings and images associated with it. This will be very useful to her when she needs to access her power place *in a situation when she doesn't feel very powerful,* such as when on the phone with Emma.

Some people have never experienced the level of confidence Lisa generally does when she's in her office. But, everyone can remember a time and place when they felt *relatively* more powerful and confident. Yours might be in a dorm room at college, on stage in a community theater play, or at the top of a mountain reached after an afternoon of strenuous rock climbing. Sometimes, it helps to discuss this idea with a friend. He or she may be able to help you remember a situation you can build into your own power place.

If, no matter how hard you look, you can't locate a time and place when you felt powerful *enough* to deal with your current situation, don't worry. Pick the best one you can find. The resource-building exercise that comes next will be of value to you.

Resource Stacking

Lisa and Tracy brainstormed a list of positive feelings, thoughts, images, beliefs and experiences they thought might be of value during a conversation with Emma. Lisa reread the list and chose three she would like to focus on, and which she had clearly experienced at one time or another in her past. The three items Lisa chose were "high energy," "feeling good about myself" and "courage."

Lisa then thought of times she'd had those experiences, and pinpointed a key element in each situation. "Courage" was easy; she'd recently seen the movie *Gandhi,* and chose a scene that had made his incredible courage real to her. For "feeling good about myself," she remembered the praise she'd received from a satisfied client. She'd also felt she'd done a slick piece of work, and the praise made her feel creative and successful (and right). For high energy she chose a movement from one of Beethoven's symphonies—Tracy said she could see Lisa come alive even as she thought about it.

135

Lisa closed her eyes and played Beethoven in her head (later she repeated this exercise with the actual record). When she felt the energy flow, she pressed her right thumb and fingers together, *associating her high-energy resource to the same trigger she'd used for her power place.* Lisa repeated this two or three times. Then, one at a time, she "installed" her other two resources in the same way. Over the next couple of weeks, she repeated the exercise whenever she got the chance, reinforcing the connection between her power place, her new resources, and her trigger.

Comment This exercise is called *resource stacking* because that is exactly what you do. Using your power place or some other solid image as a base, you associate as many other positive experiences to it as you think you might need. When you finally pit these positive resources against the negative reactions your control freak can trigger, you will need all the help you can get.

Use any resource in any form that works for you. If you are someone who doesn't visualize clearly, or who doesn't react emotionally to visual images, try using verbal affirmations, music, a piece of inspiring art work, interpretive dance or anything that may help you feel more powerful, confident, and serene. Whatever you choose, experience it as fully as you can, and then associate that experience with a trigger to help you recall it more easily the next time the going gets tough.

Verbal Countermoves

Lisa listed specific statements Emma could make on the phone that she would find upsetting to hear and difficult to answer. She was careful to write down the exact wording she thought Emma might use, and she noted the tone of voice in which the statements would be delivered. Then, for each statement, Lisa wrote out one or two ways in which, depending on the circumstances, she would like to respond (see box).

Lisa's Countermoves

Statement	*Response*
• How do you *think* I feel after my own daughter doesn't even tell me she's pregnant?	(Matching intensity) I guess you feel pretty awful, you really wanted to be first to know!
• (same statement)	(Matching intensity) Mom, I don't know how you feel. Please tell me.
• You're an insensitive young lady, do you know that?	(Gently) Maybe I am insensitive sometimes.
• *Yellow?* How could you put yellow in my grandson's room?	(*No* sarcasm or humor) Sounds like you're pretty sure we're going to have a boy.
• (same statement)	We like yellow. What color would you have preferred?

(Lisa's actual list was about 20 items long.)

Tracy and Lisa sat face to face about two and a half feet apart. Lisa took a deep breath, did one round of tension-release, and then said, "Okay." In a neutral voice, Tracy delivered the first statement on Lisa's list, and Lisa responded to it as planned. The women practiced the same statement/response until Lisa had it just right, and could respond without having to think about it.

Then Tracy added emotional intensity to her delivery: she acted angry, hurt, sarcastic or simply demanding, depending on what the particular statement called for. Lisa again responded with the countermove she'd practiced, this time matching Tracy's intensity (but not her emotion!—see page 159) as well as countering her words. They continued to practice until Lisa could respond with ease and skill, without reacting emotionally to "Emma's" behavior.

Having finished one statement, they moved on to the next. In a more advanced version of this exercise, Lisa might practice responding to a combination of demanding or critical statements, in the same way advanced aikido students practice dealing with combinations of kicks and punches, or handling several attackers at once.

Comment Psychologist Donald Meichenbaum coined the term "stress-inoculation training" to describe exercises that help people perform effectively under pressure. While the *countermoves* exercise is somewhat different from the exercises Dr. Meichenbaum describes, its purpose is similar. Lisa is being trained to react to her mother's pressure tactics with *effective countermoves*, rather than with the ineffective, fight-or-flight responses she now uses. She may never *like* the way Emma treats her—at some level she may always be hurt and disappointed by it. But she certainly can learn to respond to it more effectively.

The countermoves exercise is *not* intended to teach a complete communication strategy, and the responses Lisa picked are *not* to be taken out and used on Emma word for word. Though the sample responses presented here are fairly benign, sometimes patterns are practiced that would be totally inappropriate if employed alone or out of context.

This is an example of what we call a "piano scale exercise." Just as students practice piano scales by the hour so that eventually they will be proficient pianists, so Lisa practiced verbal "piano scales" so she might ultimately be more effective with her mother. But Lisa generally would not use a raw-form countermove on Emma (except as a last resort), just as no student would ever play scales at a piano recital. Any skills Lisa learns will be integrated into an overall communication philosophy that emphasizes alignment and collaboration. Sometimes it's not comfortable to systematically role-play the array of manipulative, hurtful moves the controllers in our lives use on us. Do it anyway. Make believe you are in the *dojo*, learning to parry kicks, punches and other fighting moves.

Putting It All Together

The nice thing about modular reprogramming is that the exercises you learn don't simply give you a way to practice individual skills; they can be combined into complex and very powerful training strategies. Furthermore, the individual exercises can be mixed and matched, and the resulting strategies tailored to the needs of individual trainees.

Dealing with a Phone Call from Emma

The following process can be done in three forms: in fantasy, in role-play, or in "real life" (with a real phone call). Ideally, all three methods are used. Here is a brief description of one variation Lisa practiced with her coach.

138

Lisa and Tracy sat facing one another; there was an old, disconnected phone on a table nearby. On Tracy's signal the exercise began.

Lisa did five or six rounds of *tension-release* to get herself as relaxed as possible. As she finished, Tracy said, "R-r-riing." She and Lisa had preplanned that Lisa would let the "phone" ring five times before answering; Lisa also planned to do this at home.

Lisa took a deep breath, exhaled, and went into her abdominal breathing; simultaneously, she replayed her oak tree visualization as clearly as possible. She'd practiced enough so that she could relax into those exercises quite rapidly.

At the fifth ring, *while continuing both the breathing and the fantasy*, Lisa picked up the receiver, put it to her ear and said, "Hello." In her best Emma voice (which she had down pat by now), Tracy loudly complained, "Lisa, where *were* you? Why did it take so long to answer? Are you hurt?" Tracy was good at her role, and Lisa felt a bit of that old twinge deep in her gut. An angry or apologetic response came to mind, and she felt her shoulders begin to tense. Then she remembered her power place, and immediately visualized being at the office—leather chair, big desk . . .

As she did so, Lisa brought the thumb and first two fingers of her right hand together, and consciously tried to recall her other resources. The hours of associating resources with power place through the trigger paid off. Into her mind flowed the sound of

Beethoven, the feeling of being praised for a job well done, and a 70mm close-up image of Gandhi, looking beatific and serene. She felt her shoulders relax, breath come in and go all the way down; and she heard her voice, relaxed and pleasant, say, "Oh, hi, Mom."

"Don't 'hi' me," sniped Tracy, and the exercise continued. But the issue was never in doubt. Lisa's natural tendency to tense up and defend herself, which quickly turned to anger and counterattack, and from there to remorse, apology and acquiescence, never had a chance to get started. Lisa practiced her countermoves, focusing on matching "Emma's" intensity without sounding angry in the process. She remembered to breathe throughout the conversation. Most of the visualizations faded away, unneeded (but on call if necessary); however, Beethoven stayed with her for the duration.

When, after a few minutes, "Emma" said, "And I guess you won't be inviting me to the christening, either," Lisa responded, "I'll invite you if you'd like to come. Let me know. Anyway, I'm off. I love you, Mom. Call you tomorrow." And she hung up.

139

The entire process took just under five minutes. Lisa and Tracy practiced twice more in role-play form; then Tracy asked her partner to perform a final visualization.

Lisa closed her eyes, and as clearly as she could she visualized a phone conversation with Emma. Tracy said, "Hear her making a demand!" and Lisa complied. After five or six seconds, Tracy said, "Okay, open your eyes. How was it?" Lisa reported being able to visualize the phone call without anxiety. They called it a session.

Comment Exercises like this always sound too pat when described in books. Please give Lisa her due—she worked for this one. Over a couple of months she put in many hours, struggled to learn several new skills, and from time to time, experienced considerable discomfort in the process. Knowing that, I was pleased, but not surprised, to see it work for her.

Frequently, change occurs much, much more quickly than it did here. Somehow, a connection with a deeper, unconscious mechanism is made, and the trainee experiences a very rapid shift. Other times, he or she simply has to grind it out.

Trainees are sometimes skeptical at first about the amount of "transfer of training" that will occur. ("Okay, I can do it in my mind. But can I take it home and use it with Fred without coming unglued?") The effects of modular reprogramming usually transfer extremely well to real-world situations.

Other Methods

Through practice and persistence in learning a specific reprogramming strategy, Lisa successfully broke free of the control and accommodation cycles she and her mother were trapped in. However, what works for Lisa may not be right for you. To repeat, it is important to fit any blueprint for change to the individual doing the changing. Here are some additional ideas you might try.

Start a Feel-Better Campaign

Spend more time with upbeat, noncontrolling people. Cultivate new friends who fit that description, or join a support group. Learn new skills. Take on a complete new project. Go on a diet. Start and stick to an exercise program. Get involved in community services.

Find something, *anything* that makes you feel better about yourself, more capable or more in charge of your own life, and pursue it. Even though the activities you choose may not be remotely related to the situation which is causing you problems, the resulting self-confidence and self-sufficiency automatically reduce your vulnerability to controlling people.

Reframe Unproductive Viewpoints

Many of us feed, or at least have trouble dousing, the fires set by control freaks because of our own preconceived points of view. Fortunately thoughts are merely thoughts—they are not etched in stone. You can change your mental pictures, replacing them with ideas and attitudes that enable you to feel safe, secure and in control of your own life, but which do not cost you as much. You can reframe reality—not change it, mind you—by changing the way you look at it, altering your viewpoint to reduce the emotional charge of various situations, and increasing your personal power as a result.

Sometimes you can reframe the control freak as well. Try to picture people who intimidate you in different settings or doing different things. Think of that hard-nosed executive diapering a baby, or that perfectly-put-together friend changing a tire in the rain. When you deal with controllers whom you've put on pedestals, run through a list of things you probably do better than they do—getting organized, baking bread, relaxing, finding shortcuts or appreciating the changing seasons.

Don't Take It Personally Controllers *are* directing their tactics at you, and they *are* stirring up emotions and creating conditions that upset and thwart you. But it does not help you to look at the situation that way. Instead of viewing the controlling people in your life as manipulative, power-hungry bad guys who are dead set on making you miserable, try looking at them as robots with glitches in their programming.

They are acting out of habit, desperately—and, more often than not, ineffectively—trying to manage their emotions, compensate for their insecurities, and feel safe, comfortable and in control. In fact, their behavior may have nothing to do with you per se. So, *practice coming up with alternate explanations for their actions.* Maybe she had a fight with her boyfriend; or maybe he's having a bad day; or maybe she's trying to win points with her boss.

141

See Problems as Opportunities You can also train yourself to *view problems as opportunities.* Conflicts, chaos, impasses and the like become less threatening when you perceive them as a chance to learn about yourself, practice new skills, or prove that you can cope without falling apart at the seams. For instance, the next time your hypercritical spouse starts in on you, don't groan, "Oh, God, here we go again!" Instead, take a deep breath and say to yourself, Okay—now I have an opportunity to practice some of the things I learned from that book!"

Manage Your Emotions

Most of us get so worried or worked up about upcoming contacts with control freaks, that we unwittingly play right into their hands. You may still feel so uncomfortable during your encounters with controlling individuals that you rush through them, saying and doing anything you can think of to get the situation over with as quickly as possible and to relieve the anger, guilt, outrage, confusion, anxiety. However, what we *need* to do in order to deal more effectively with control freaks is to *tolerate* unsettling emotions—to feel them without giving in to them, to be aware of them but remain in control of our actions.

Visualization Our distress during control interactions is not only a reaction to the situation itself, but also the result of our worst-case scenarios. We see ourselves getting fired and ending up destitute and homeless, being disowned by our families, losing custody of our children, creating a scandal that will haunt us for the rest of our days. In a variation on Lisa's use of creative visualization to deal with Emma, you can use your anxiety-provoking predictions to prepare yourself for reasonable negative outcomes, thereby increasing your tolerance for uncertainty, conflict and psychological distress.

142

The next time you know you will be facing a stressful situation or plan to try a new technique for dealing with a control freak, visualize the upcoming interaction as if you were watching it on videotape. Make your visualization as detailed as possible and as soon as you feel your anxiety level rising, stop the tape. Identify the barrier you encountered: your mother gave you "that look"; your friend yelled, "I don't have to stick around and take this abuse." Focus on what you are feeling, thinking, remembering, but most of all, *predicting.* Start the tape again, take a deep breath, and continue the encounter, following it through to a negative outcome. Indulge your worst-case fantasies, then stop and change the tape. Replay the scene, visualizing yourself using reprogrammed behavior, and *having it work.* Practice the visualization and contingency-planning process until you have, in your mind's eye, gotten through *both* the negative and positive situations. The awareness that you can actually cope with and survive either consequence makes it easier for you to take risks, and affirms the very real potential of a positive outcome.

Affirmations Affirmations deliberately planted in your mind provide encouragement and remind you of your strengths, goals and positive attributes. Develop a list of two dozen affirmations by completing sentences beginning with the words "I can . . . ," "I deserve . . . ," "I am proud of . . . ," or by copying short upbeat, inspirational passages from books, poems or songs.

Read them aloud, slowly, listening to your own words and

letting them sink in. Then read them at least once a day every day and whenever you are facing someone or something that typically arouses anxiety or activates your programming. This repetition is a must. You are dealing with negative thoughts and feelings that took years to develop, so it takes lots of practice to get these new, more realistic, self-enhancing ideas to take hold.

A word of caution here. Affirmations are useful tools, but to work properly they should be combined with other training aids. Using affirmations to *cover up* unresolved conflicts and automatic reactions is a bit like painting a rusty fence without taking the rust off first. The fence may look better for a while, but the change won't last.

Simple Acceptance Although you can often use your emotions as strategic tools sometimes it's best to sit with them and let them run their course. Tell yourself that it's okay to feel angry or discounted or afraid—not preferable, but acceptable. **143** Feelings have a beginning, middle and an end, and no matter how uncomfortable or unsettling they may be, eventually they *will* subside.

Know Your Limits

Acquaint yourself with your nonnegotiable limits. Take some time to identify the *least* you could accept from a person or situation in order to live with an outcome and maintain your integrity. This should be more than you are getting now but less than a pie-in-the-sky best-case fantasy. Be specific. Clarity in this area gives you a solid foundation on which to stand during control interactions. Knowing what really matters to you makes it possible for you to commit yourself to doing what it takes to resolve conflicts constructively.

Follow-up

1. After finishing Chapters 7–9, come back and retake the Questionnaire. Use the results to fill out a Reprogramming Worksheet.

2. Use the Worksheet to design a program like Lisa's that will help you reduce some of the automatic reactions you have to a controlling person in your life.

OBSERVATION AND ALIGNMENT

RIDING THE TIGER IN THE DIRECTION IT'S GOING

Developing self-awareness is an ongoing, never-ending process. Although you certainly don't need to become perpetual navel-gazers who spend so much time analyzing themselves that they never get around to accomplishing anything, I firmly believe that you can never know too much about yourself, your basic programming and your typical responses to difficult situations. When you are tuned in and self-aware, you can identify self-defeating thoughts and behavior patterns before they get in your way and lead you right back into a control trap.

As you become more adept at tapping your internal resources; and tolerating unsettling emotions, you will be less likely to switch to autopilot when dealing with control freaks. The more you practice breathing, centering yourself, visualizing yourself in stressful situations and so on, the calmer you will become. Eventually, you will be able to stay centered throughout entire control interactions, sidestepping the various traps and pitfalls that once ensnared you. With growing self-confidence, you will be willing to take chances, try new alternatives and look for creative, caring, nonjudgmental solutions to control problems.

This chapter describes one such option: the aikido alternative, which was introduced in Chapter 5. Although it will not eliminate conflict from your life or prevent control freaks from trying to control you, the aikido approach will help you meet your needs without alienating other people or getting clobbered yourself.

You accomplish this feat by *paying attention and gathering information, using that information to align and build rapport with the controller and then gently steering the interaction in the direction you would prefer it to go.* Although the aikido approach will be described here as if it were a step-by-step process, it is really circular and quite fluid. Keep in mind that during an actual interaction, you are *always* paying attention, gathering information, and, aligning. And although this chapter teaches alignment and the next one redirecting, in real life you'll move back and forth between these phases and often will use them simultaneously.

Observation

When you use the aikido alternative, you begin in a centered, neutral position, doing nothing but paying attention and collecting data. Rather than trying to make something happen or to prevent something from happening, try to find out what *is* happening—learn as much as you can about the controller's position, needs, methods and point of view. Try to be as detached and objective as possible, letting words and actions that typically get to you simply roll off your back.

To avoid getting hooked by the other person's bullying or manipulative behavior, practice centering and empowerment techniques such as those described in the last chapter. Alternatively (or in addition), some people find it helpful to think of

> This is a good time to practice a variation on the breathing exercise you learned in the last chapter. As you pay careful attention to the controller's words and behavior, also be aware of your breathing. Keep it relaxed and regular. Let yourself breathe a bit deeper and more slowly than you normally do. Then redirect any tension or emotion you feel into your breathing, releasing it on exhalation. Breathe out the anger and stress, stay relaxed, and continue to observe. Your breathing acts something like the escape valve on a pressure cooker, literally giving you a vent for emotional reactions that otherwise might build up and get in your way.

themselves as computers receiving input to be filed away for future use. Others mentally step back and view the situation as if it were happening to someone else.

Focus on the controller's verbal and nonverbal behavior. Tune out extraneous noises and intrusive thoughts. Ignore any quirks that are not relevant to the immediate situation. Listen carefully to what the other person is saying even if you do not like how she says it or are convinced she's dead wrong. Mentally track the conversation, summarizing it in your mind as it goes along and tagging the points you want to address later. At any given moment, you should be able to "feed back" the control freak's last sentence or two, and be able to describe the important components of his nonverbal behavior.

Sometimes it helps to silently talk to yourself, especially when the technique you're trying to employ is new to you. The internal dialogue might go something like this:

"He said, 'As you well know . . .' but since this is the first I've heard about it, he may just be trying to keep me from questioning him. He says he wants me to start taking more responsibility around here. I'll have to find out what he means by that. Now he's driving home his point by leaning forward and aiming his index finger at me. He's leaning back again, folding his hands, waiting for a response."

Here are some of the things you might look for during an interaction with a control freak.

Needs, Motives, Payoffs

In Chapter 4, we learned that unfulfilled needs underlie nearly all control behavior. (Sometimes these needs haven't got much to do with what the controller seems to be trying to achieve. For instance, your spouse may nag at you about an undone chore because he or she is lonely or wants attention.) When you use the aikido approach, your goal is to help the controller *fulfill at least some of his or her needs in a way that doesn't keep you from satisfying some of your own.* Try to figure out what needs, fears or expectations might be the driving force behind the other person's controlling behavior.

> The single most important question you can ask yourself when trying to figure out how to deal with a controller is: *"What does this person need from me that will reduce his need or desire to control me.* A great many needs can underlie control behavior; many of these you may be unable or unwilling to address. But there may be some you can serve, without materially reducing the quality of your own life.

For instance, is the person who uses third-party referencing (*"I* don't have a problem with the contract, but Bill won't sign it until you change this clause") afraid of being held accountable or thought of as the bad guy? Does she lack self-confidence and think that if the objection came from her, you wouldn't take it seriously? Perhaps she is trying to avoid a direct confrontation. Careful observation will reveal which of these incentives is likely to be motivating her.

147

When your boss checks up on you or your father plays "District Attorney" and tries to build an airtight case against you, does he seem anxious or angry, insecure or sublimely self-confident, interested in accomplishing a tangible goal or enhancing his image? Does your meddling mother-in-law, tantrum-throwing ten-year-old, pontificating neighbor or overly helpful friend want to:

- be right?

- express anger or some other emotion?

- have you agree with her point of view or recognize how valuable she is?

- avoid embarrassment, humiliation or loss of face?

- feel honored, appreciated, or understood?

- make sure no unforeseen circumstances slow him down or get in his way?

- get some attention?

- impress you (or his boss, his staff, his parents or his kids)?

Although you can never know exactly what drives another person, if you pay attention you can get a reasonably accurate sense of what payoffs other people are trying to obtain by controlling you. Then you can begin to think about ways to help them either achieve those payoffs or *reduce their need for them*, without sacrificing your own needs and goals in the process.

Specific Control Tactics

Be able to describe the controller's behavior in terms of the specific effects they have on you, according to the guidelines offered in Chapter 2. Do you feel overpowered? Undermined? Short-circuited? Does her control strategy include takeover? Intimidation? Deception? Disconnection? Prepare to deal with specific combinations of these tactics, as skilled controllers rarely use them one at a time.

148

A word of caution here. When you are dealing with a controller who is well known to you, it is easy to assume she will use the same tactic or style she used last time. In fact, prior knowledge can be extremely useful—people do tend to behave consistently, at least in similar situations. However, don't go to sleep! Only unskilled control freaks always use the same style. The good ones will mix it up on you. The minute you think you've got them pegged, they'll come at you from a new angle and have you drawn and quartered before you even realize the game changed. No matter how much you think you know about the controller, there is no substitute for paying attention to his or her actual words and actions in the here and now.

Timing

Consider the timing of certain remarks. Does the controller open fire or bring up complex, emotionally charged subjects when you are busy, on your way out the door, or talking about something else? Did you get ambushed? You did if you were at a cocktail party conversing with a small group of casual acquaintances when a close friend said, "You have to tell them about the time you . . ." and insisted that you recount an embarrassing experience which you had told your friend to keep secret. You did if your boss turned to you during a staff meeting and said, "I'll let you explain why you are backing my idea." The controller caught you off guard and put you on the spot, making it virtually impossible for you to do anything but what he wanted.

Emotional Hooks Learn to recognize what the control freak is indirectly saying: the implications, presuppositions and distortions that are carried in the *structure* of certain message forms. You're most vulnerable to these pesky little creatures when you don't realize they are being used on you. Skilled controllers can weave them into incredibly subtle and complex patterns—many times you only realize you've been manipulated (again) after you've agreed to babysit for your daughter-in-law and your headache has come back. On the other hand, if you recognize these patterns in time, most of them can be defused rather easily. Here are some examples.

When he says, "If you really loved me [If you cared about your job], then you would iron my shirts [then you would not mind working overtime]," he is implying that not ironing his shirts proves you don't love him or not wanting to work overtime proves that you are disloyal or uncommitted to your job. He wants you to prove to him that what he is implying is not true—by doing things his way.

When she says, "Don't you even care about your kids [or my feelings or the department's reputation]," she is implying that you don't and you should. She wants you to feel guilty about a specific situation or ashamed of yourself in general. So do people who say, "Even *you* should be able to do this [or have figured that out by now]." They are implying that there is something wrong with you and that not doing or figuring out what they think you should is further proof of your deficiencies. They are urging you to try harder to live up to their expectations.

Finally, certain controlling persons in your life might say, "*Some* wives [or husbands, supervisors, etc.] would be angry at you, [never forgive you, leave you, or fire you] for doing that." There is a whole series of unspoken messages imbedded in that statement. The speakers are implying that you have blown it and anyone else would blast you for it. But because they are superior, supremely tolerant beings, they will overlook your unforgivable behavior. They expect you to feel like the lowest life form imaginable and to repay their favor in some way.

A more extensive (though by no means complete) list of semantic control patterns is presented in the accompanying box. See if you can recognize the implication or presupposition im-

149

bedded in each one. For additional information on this fascinating topic, read one of Suzette Haden Elgin's books on verbal self-defense, or Eric Berne's older, but by no means outdated, book *Games People Play*. A brief discussion of each is presented at the end of the section.

TWELVE COMMON EMOTIONAL HOOKS

1. If it weren't for me you'd still be in the secretarial pool.

2. Oh sure you remembered our anniversary. So how come you're late for dinner?

3. I'm sure if you really think about it you'll agree with me.

4. Which night can you work late, Wednesday or Thursday?

5. I should have known you'd get a dent in our new car. It's my fault for letting you drive it!

6. You really shouldn't let the boss take advantage of your good nature.

7. I don't mean to be critical but saying that made you look like a fool.

8. You aren't actually planning to wear *that* dress to the party, are you?

9. You always have to have the last word!

10. If it weren't for you, I'd have finished college.

11. Personally, I have no problem with your bringing the kids, but I think it will upset some of the other guests.

12. Go ahead. Why should I mind staying home alone *again* tonight?

Nonverbal Signals In addition to what is being said or implied, pay attention to how messages are being conveyed and the behavior that accompanies them. Research has shown that up to 70 percent of the information we receive is communicated to us nonverbally. So tune into all channels and absorb the data transmitted to you through body language, facial expressions, eye contact and physical signs of emotion such as reddened faces or rapid breathing. Take mental notes on the other person's tone of voice, pitch and intensity. Is he stammering, repeating himself, beating around the bush? Are there long pauses between thoughts or a rapid rushed quality to his speech? Does the conversation suddenly change directions? When you are talking, does the controller fidget, avoid eye contact, sigh, or otherwise make his lack of interest, skepticism or inattentiveness quite noticeable?

Double Messages and Contradictions When verbal and nonverbal messages contradict each other and you have no solid evidence to tell you which message conveys the controller's true meaning, the signals coming through on the nonverbal channel are usually more reliable. However, all messages and especially nonverbal signals should be interpreted tentatively. They do not mean the same thing all of the time or for all people. Your mother may be frowning because she is angry at you, or because she has indigestion. When your husband folds his arms across his chest, it may mean that he is not receptive to your ideas. But it may also mean that his arms are tired or that he is actually listening intently. Consequently, you can interpret specific body-language cues only in combination with other information.

151

If you haven't interacted with someone often enough to pick up patterns in his or her behavior, don't jump to conclusions. Collect more data and test the information you gather against anything you already know to be true. And while you're at it, make sure that your own mental filter is not distorting the signals you are receiving.

Your Own Biases and Presuppositions Throughout your interactions with controlling individuals, guard against any tendency on your part to raise the emotional ante or label the other person a control freak simply because you don't like what is happening, or because you have a preexisting viewpoint or position on the matter. The words you are hearing and the nonverbal cues you are observing may or may not mean that the other person is trying to control you. So periodically stop and ask yourself, "Whose problem is this?" More specifically:

- "Am I assuming that this person's attitudes, feelings, communication style and preferences are the same as my own, or that they should be?" People are different, and it is important to take those differences into account. Coming from someone else, certain words and actions may have an entirely different meaning than they would have if they came from you.

- "Am I anticipating rejection, criticism, anger or a guilt trip and looking for signs to prove that my prediction is coming true?" This "confirmatory bias" (a natural tendency to pay attention to data that supports our own viewpoint, while ignoring information that may not support it) can make mountains out of molehills and attribute meanings to other people's behavior that they never intended to convey.

152

- "Have I magnified this interaction into a do-or-die situation?" When you think that your job, marriage, sanity or entire future is on the line, your objectivity goes right out the window. It is replaced by desperation, anxiety or stubborn determination to wrestle the reins of control out of the control freak's hands.

- "Was I feeling particularly vulnerable before this interaction got under way?" Your physical or emotional state can make you more sensitive to certain remarks and more susceptible to certain control tactics.

Even the most extreme control freaks won't try to control you all of the time. Often, they may be friendly, docile, kind or understanding, getting something from you just isn't on the agenda that day. If there's no immediate conflict between their needs and your own, and nothing you're about to bring up will set them off, then by all means enjoy the moment. But never assume they have somehow seen the error of their ways and will treat you with honor and respect from here on out. Stay alert: many control freaks have hair triggers, and things could change at any moment. You may say the wrong thing and get hit with a control move you never saw coming. For that matter, you may already be on the receiving end of an maneuver you simply haven't recognized yet. Or the controller may be skillfully setting you up for a play he or she intends to make later on.

Data-Collecting Tips

1. Listen for feelings as well as facts.

2. Be aware of your feelings as well. But don't allow them to get the better of you. Picture yourself placing those feelings into an imaginary In box. Tell yourself you'll get back to them as soon as you can.

3. Take notes if it's possible and appropriate to do so.

4. Don't jump to conclusions. As you track incoming data, always think in terms of what it *might* mean rather than what it *must* mean.

5. Remember that you can think faster than the other person can talk. You won't be overwhelmed by an onslaught of incoming information.

6. Be involved. Nod. Maintain eye contact. Ask questions. Periodically reflect back to the speaker the messages you are receiving.

7. When you're receiving, just receive. Try not to plan your reply while the other person is transmitting information to you.

8. Remember to breathe and stay calm, centered and grounded. *Don't take it personally.* No matter what the control freak says or does, it is simply data, information about the control freak, which may be useful to you later on.

Practice, Practice, Practice

You don't have to wait for a seminar or a control freak to come along in order to practice observation skills. As a matter of fact, while classroom learning can be useful, the atmosphere is often so artificial that the skills you practice don't transfer very well to the real world. On the other hand, practicing new skills on actual control freaks can get you in trouble very quickly. It's often better to practice in real-world but *low-risk* situations before trying to use them when there's a lot on the line. Fortunately, you can practice observing anywhere.

Remind yourself to pay attention to waitresses, salespeople, and co-workers. Can you tell if they are at the beginning or the end of their shift? Do they seem tired, keyed up, burned out, full of enthusiasm? Find five verbal or nonverbal cues that give you that impression. Ask them an unexpected question—nothing intrusive or offensive, just something simple such as their name, how they like their job, or where they got their earrings. Try to make five educated guesses about them based on the way they respond.

Have a friend tell you about two experiences, one the absolute truth, the other a complete fabrication. Try to guess which one is which. On what did you base your decision?

Watch a TV soap opera, situation comedy or talk show with several friends or relatives. Pick one character (or talk-show guest) whom all of you will observe. During the commercial break compare notes on what you learned from watching and listening to your subject. Notice the differences in perception. Pick a different character and repeat the process, only this time turn off the sound.

154

TWELVE COMMON EMOTIONAL HOOKS—COMMENTS

Some of the semantic patterns controllers use to hook you are complex, and can be taken in various ways. Here is *one* possible interpretation for each of the statements in the accompanying box.

1. An *indebtedness* ploy. "I did you an important favor, therefore you owe me something in return." This pattern controls by inducing guilt or misplaced responsibility. (Although it's fine to return favors, you don't *owe* the controller anything unless you agreed to the exchange beforehand.)

2. Sarcasm followed by imbedded criticism and what is called a *causal implication.* "I think you're lying about remembering our anniversary, otherwise you would have been on time for dinner. I think I'll zing you with a trap question."

3. *Assumed agreement,* laced with the threat of criticism.

"I'm obviously right, and you would be stupid not to agree. You're not stupid . . . are you?"

4. *Forced choice.* "There's no question about whether or not you will work late—it's only a matter of picking the night."

5. Double *imbedded criticism.* In this variation, the controller talks about herself when it's clear she really means you. "I should have known" means *"You* should have known"; "It's *my* fault" means "It's *your* fault."

6. A *presupposition* ("The boss is taking advantage of you" followed by *judgment* ("You're doing wrong to let him").

7. *Disclaimers* like this one often telegraph the statement's real meaning. ("I *do* mean to be critical—I just don't want you to call me on it.")

8. *Imbedded criticism.* Questions are often used this way. The underlying meaning is "I don't like that dress" or "You should know that dress is inappropriate for this party."

9. Words like "always" and "never" are called *categorical imperatives.* More accurate (and less loaded): "You seem to want the last word a lot, and I feel frustrated."

10. *Blame.* "I wish I'd finished college [or "I don't like how my life turned out"] and I don't want to take responsibility for the choice, so I think I'll lay it on you."

11. *Third-party referencing,* in this case in order to pass the buck. "I don't want you to bring your kids, but I don't want to have to tell you that."

12. *Denial* and *double message,* intended to induce guilt. The controller's words say one thing, his voice tonality and body language something else entirely. "I'm upset that you go out a lot. I want you to stay home but don't think I should have to ask." Or "I don't think asking would do any good."

Caution: These are only interpretations *and will not be right for everyone!* Some people just talk this way. In that case, your job would be to mentally *decode* the statement (see Chapter 8, Advanced Tactics) rather than stopping to clarify or deflect it.

Alignment

Some of you have never had any trouble figuring out what the controlling people in your life were up to. It's what you do with that information that causes problems. You use it to talk yourself into giving in to control freaks and to get your interaction over with as quickly as possible. Or you use it against control freaks, turning their words and actions into weapons and launching counterattacks.

With the aikido alternative, however, you must forgo the opportunity to be a martyr who sacrifices herself to serve others or a hero who lays down his life in the heat of a battle. Instead, you use a variety of "secondary control tactics" (see box) to create the beginnings of harmony and rapport between yourself and controllers. Like a ballroom dancer, you follow their lead. You get on the same wavelength, speak the same language, use the same metaphors, empathize with them. In other words, you align.

Secondary Control Tactics

People who use what researchers call "secondary control" try to maximize the quality of their lives by adapting to the people and situations around them (rather than trying to get those people and situations to change). Secondary control tactics include giving in, empathizing, making the best of a bad situation, reframing a problem as an opportunity (rather than trying to make the problem go away), and so on. There seems to be strong cultural differences here: Westerners tend to favor direct, assertive, primary control tactics, whereas residents of Japan and other Asian cultures place a much higher value on secondary control.

Alignment itself is a secondary control tactic (actually a set of many tactics), but aikido is not. The aikido master aligns as a part of a larger effort that ultimately results in primary control: he or she aligns in order to redirect, or lead. However, a built-in bias against secondary control still makes it difficult for some people to learn and use aikido skills.

An Alternative, Not an Edict

Aligning means allowing, even encouraging, controlling behavior to continue temporarily. You simply may not be willing to do that. It is your indisputable right *not* to have to put up with inappropriate or abusive behavior, no matter how strategic it may be to do so. Be willing to exercise that right!

If you are unwilling or unable to tolerate another second of yelling, threats, criticism, pouting or anything else, then *don't.* Stop the interaction immediately by walking away from it or using one of the other disconnection tactics described in Chapter 5. Or tell the controller that you will use one of those measures if he does not discontinue the behavior. The limit-setting tactics described in the next chapter may also be helpful.

If you decide that you *can* tolerate whatever the control freak is doing for a while longer (or your circumstances are such that you could not stop him even if you wanted to), then it may be time to learn to align. The balance of this chapter describes variations on three of the most basic and useful alignment tactics—*matching, clarifying* and *strategic yielding.*

Matching

This technique involves blending in with the controller, mirroring his position or communication style and temporarily accepting the "rightness" of his point of view. Sometimes this is referred to as "learning to speak the other person's language." When, for example, you visit a foreign land, you will be accepted and trusted much more quickly if you can converse with the residents in their native tongue. Precisely the same principle applies when the "languages" in question are made up of nonverbal signals, cultural idioms and differences in personal style.

157

Match Speech Patterns You can do this verbally by mirroring the rhythm and cadence of the controller's speech. Increase your pace for someone who talks rapidly and decrease it for someone who drawls or drags out each sentence, placing emphasis on the same words. Try to use the same jargon, idioms, phraseology and, in some cases, words the controller uses (for example, if she calls flavored carbonated water "pop," then you call it pop). If the controller's speech is relatively jargon-free, then yours should be as well.

Match Communication Style Be direct with someone who is direct with you; be a bit more tangential with people who use an indirect style. Try counting on your fingers while giving reasons to someone who uses logic as a control tactic. If the other person is discussing what he sees as the facts of the matter, you talk about facts as well (say "I think" or "I understand," rather than "I feel" or "I believe"). If the other person is being emotional, reflect his feelings and share feelings of your own. Consider cultural differences. Some Americans can't hear anything softer than a slammed door while someone from Japan might be offended by a simple, assertive "no."

158

Match Physical Movements and Body Language You might want to mirror the controller's movements or body language. (Make sure you do it subtly enough that the controller doesn't recognize what you're doing.) Rather than backing away from someone who has just aggressively moved toward you (as most of us are inclined to do) stand your ground or take a step in her direction. (Make sure your movements don't look aggressive when using this one—use an open body posture and a pleasant smile.)

On the other hand, if a more indirect controller tries to put some distance between you, and the situation allows, give him even more room. For instance, the best way to align with someone who pouts or sulks is to leave him alone for a few days (or years!). If you *must* communicate with him, do so as briefly and with as little energy as possible. "Chasing" a pouter (spending a lot of energy cheering him up or trying to persuade him not to pout) is not only a waste of your time, but will also reinforce the pouting pattern.

Match Intensity Matching intensity can be particularly effective. This is sometimes called being "as present" as the controller. Use an assertive body posture, an energetic voice, emphatic movements, and a lot of eye contact when dealing with someone who is coming on strong. (You may also increase your volume if you can do so without sounding angry. Be very careful with this tactic: no matter how you sound, many people associate a raised voice with strong emotion. See the accompanying box.)

Speak more softly and gently to passive, "helpless" or seemingly uninterested controllers. They require a more delicate touch. And, as in the previous example, say as little as possible to someone who withdraws, clams up, or otherwise disconnects. As a rule, we talk far too much to people who are intent upon avoiding conversations with us.

159

Matching Intensity vs. Matching Emotion

Matching intensity does *not* mean matching emotion. You don't have to act sad to deal with a sad controller, and I suggest you don't match anger with anger unless you want to start a fight. Intensity-matching lets the controller know you are willing to hang in there no matter what happens, and that you are strong enough and concerned enough to do so. This increases the chances for eventual collaboration between you. However, pretending to feel angry or sad in order to foster some kind of fake empathy is a bad idea, and has nothing to do with intensity-matching.

Clarifying

This alignment technique brings hidden agendas out into the open and is particularly useful for dealing with controllers who use emotional exploitation and other indirect tactics such as double messages, implications, broad generalizations, global accusations and vaguely defined demands. For instance, you might ask the controller to give you specific examples of a behavior he is criticizing:

BOSS: Your attitude stinks.

WORKER: Specifically, what did I say or do that convinced you
           I had an attitude problem?

You can request more precise instructions . . .

WIFE: I'm not your maid. When are you going to start
           sharing some of the responsibility around here?

HUSBAND: Exactly what could I do to share the responsibility?

. . . or try to verify that you understood what the other person
meant.

ELLEN: If you cared about our friendship, you wouldn't flit
           from table to table when we go out together.

BEVERLY: Do you really believe that I don't care about our
           friendship?

160

You can even ask for something you are afraid you might get,
bring up a sensitive topic first, or say what you suspect the other
person is thinking. For instance, you might be afraid that your
supervisor, who is walking rapidly toward your office, is about to
blast you for missing a deadline. Get up, get to her before she
reaches your office, and say, "Do you have a minute? I need to
talk to you about that late report." You may still get blasted, but
you almost certainly will be in a stronger position than if you'd
waited for her. You will have presented a more take-charge image, and will have aligned with her need to deal with the missed
deadline. (However, be warned: this tactic works a lot better
after the first missed deadline than it does after the tenth!)

Clarification strategies coax controllers to lay their cards on
the table and provide you with additional information that may
prove useful later on. In addition, controllers will feel listened to
—you will be aligning with their need to be taken seriously.
Finally, in the face of your apparent cooperation, they may run
out of steam more rapidly than they would have if you had
resisted their control.

Most clarification tactics work best in combination with
matching. That is, match the other person's intensity and style
when you ask for clarification. If you question or paraphrase in a
flat, neutral voice, the other person will quickly begin to feel
"techniqued." And he or she may be very quick to call you on

it! If you ever hear the angry retort "Don't you use those damn techniques on me!" it probably means you've been using verbal alignment skills, but have not matched the controller's intensity or aligned effectively on other nonverbal channels.

Finally, and most important—*never* clarify in a sarcastic or angry tone of voice. Even subtle differences in tone quality can dramatically change the message conveyed by your words. The question "Do you really believe I don't care about our friendship?" means one thing when delivered in an interested, concerned manner, and quite another when asked sarcastically. The latter is most emphatically *not* alignment. Generally such queries convey disbelief, and are taken as an attack.

Strategic Yielding

This is perhaps the most difficult of the three alignment techniques presented here. Trading a short-term loss for the possibility of a long-term gain is a foreign, perhaps even offensive idea for most of us. We would rather fight than yield, and are loath to concede a battle even when it could help us win the war. And so instead, we lose.

161

Aikido masters know better. For instance, when they realize they are about to be thrown, they adapt. They *choose to be thrown,* in a way that not only does the least damage to them but also leaves them in the best position to resume the battle and reengage their opponent. Of course, they would prefer not to be thrown at all. But, having lost that choice, they do the next best thing: they *utilize* the temporary setback, and turn it into a long-term advantage. You can do that too.

Living to Fight Another Day The first step involves learning to recognize—and being willing to admit—that an interaction has reached the point of diminishing returns. Do an honest cost/benefit analysis. Will continuing to struggle cost you more time, trouble, or aggravation than it's worth? If so, consider another alternative.

For example, Drew recognized that no matter how valiantly he resisted his father-in-law's control, Carl would continue to meddle and give unsolicited advice. What's more, his battles were disrupting family gatherings, upsetting his wife, and making him look as pigheaded as Carl. It was a waste of time and energy to kick up a fuss each and every time Carl interfered.

Besides, some of his advice was useful. So Drew decided, with a great deal of ambivalence, to learn the art of strategic yielding.

There may be times when you come to that realization as well: resistance isn't working, and/or isn't worth the cost. You may recognize that the other person has a point or is better suited to call the shots in a particular situation than you are. Let him! Go along with him. Admit to him that he might be right. (See Chapter 8.) Emphasize the areas where you agree. Consciously choose to give in—because it is in your best interest to do so *for the time being*. Be patient. Using secondary control tactics, work toward that time when you will be in a better position to redirect or lead.

Going with What You Get   Try eliciting *more* reasons from a rational eroder who bombards you with logical explanations. Or you might ask someone who gives unsolicited advice for additional suggestions. If an overly helpful controller reorganizes your files, cleans out your linen closet, or plans the itinerary for your vacation, why not get more help? Only this time make it help you need. "While you're at it, could you make up an index so we all know where things are filed?" you might ask your file organizer. "You know, I could use some help with the kitchen cabinets too," you might say to the linen closet cleaner. You might even playfully add, "Do you do windows?" (If you try this, *don't* sound sarcastic. Deliver the additional requests sincerely, as if butter wouldn't melt in your mouth. And if the other person says, "Yes," be prepared to get out the squeegee.) The point is *not* to resist the controlling behavior, which inevitably prompts the controller to raise the stakes and try even harder to take command.

Dealing with Emotional Reactions   First, don't make the common mistake of thinking that emotional outbursts must be stopped. Your immediate inclination may to tell an angry person to calm down or to say "Hold on now. Let's talk about this rationally." Don't do it, except as a last resort. (How do *you* feel when someone says to you, "Calm down. Let's talk about this rationally?") Chances are that trying to block an expression of emotion or make the controller wrong for feeling it will only get her angrier.

You will almost always be better off going along with the tantrum thrower and saying something like "Obviously this is really upsetting you. Specifically what went wrong?'' Remember to match intensity (but not the anger!) so that the controller knows you are not placating her but rather are sincerely concerned. If, while staying problem-focused, you give her implicit permission to vent her anger, she may eventually calm down and be more able to attack the underlying issue (rather than you).

Similarly, when someone cries, sulks or nonverbally conveys his discontent, your immediate inclination may be to switch to "fix-it" mode in order to avoid *your* discomfort. On one level sincerely wanting to help and on another wanting to lessen the impact the other person's pain has on you, you quickly try to put a lid on his feelings, to control what he is dumping on you by apologizing, telling him not to feel that way, leaving the scene or trying to make things better.

Instead, try giving the crier a tissue, nonverbally letting him know that it is okay to cry. Then wait quietly for him to compose himself. With the sulker or someone who is giving you the silent treatment, make one attempt to have her tell you what is bothering her. Then withdraw. Wait quietly. Walk away. Keep yourself busy with other tasks until you notice signs that the other person is coming around.

163

Tools of the Trade

Here are four basic communication skills that come in handy when aligning with control freaks:

Paraphrase Paraphrasing involves summarizing the other person's position or message in your own words. It is the most effective verbal method for verifying that you understand what is being conveyed to you, letting other people know you are with them and encouraging them to continue moving in the direction they are already going.

There are many variations, some of which are quite complicated. For alignment purposes, learn to use the *summary* form of paraphrase first—it is straightforward, and the other person is unlikely to accuse you of using a communication technique. Begin by saying something like "I want to make sure I'm following you . . ." or more simply, "In other words . . ."

COLLEAGUE:	You really blew it on the Johnson deal. You overcharged them! You're going to be in deep trouble when Mr. Howard gets back! When will you ever learn?
EMPLOYEE:	Let me make sure I understand you. As far as you're concerned we lost Johnson specifically because my price was too high. And you're pretty sure the boss will see it the same way.

Another form, often used with shorter statements (and for variety) begins with phrases like "It sounds like . . . or simply "So you think/feel/believe/(etc.)" This form can sound accusatory, so be sure to use a gentle, interested manner.

MARK:	If you don't change your plans and go to the Caribbean with me, I'll know you're not the woman for me.
JULIE:	It sounds like you see our vacation plans as the issue that will make or break our relationship.

Questions can also be used to summarize, although sometimes the controller is left feeling a bit "interviewed," or put on the spot. Finally, advanced forms of paraphrase are used to clarify indirect messages (see example on page 159) and when responding to certain emotional hooks.

Acknowledgment This is anything you do or say to let the speaker know you are listening. Nonverbal acknowledgments include nodding, maintaining eye contact, or periodically saying "Uh-huh."

True acknowledgment doesn't imply agreement, though of course you can agree and acknowledge at the same time. Paraphrasing automatically acknowledges (for obvious reasons), and sometimes acknowledgment takes the form of a very short paraphrase. Some people find it useful to occasionally echo the speaker, repeating a certain word or phrase exactly as it has been spoken.

WIFE:	I know you couldn't care less, but my day was absolutely horrendous.
HUSBAND:	(Matching her tone) Horrendous?

In addition, you can acknowledge points of agreement—"You're right, I have been awfully busy lately," or "You have a point. I didn't return your call the other day." Giving a qualified agreement—"You might be right about that" or "I can see how you might feel that way"—can also be a powerful alignment strategy (see Chapter 8, page 173).

Specificity Questions These help you obtain additional information, and communicate interest in the other person's point of view. "Specifically, what do you mean by 'not stopping to think things through'?" or "Exactly what happened to upset you?" They can help you clarify vague demands or general comments—"Exactly what kind of figures are you looking for and by when do you need them?" or "Specifically, what do you want to see or hear from me that would let you know I have done my homework for this project?" And you can use them to elicit "more of the same" from a control freak as well—"What other reasons can you give me for changing my mind?" or "Is there anything else you can tell me that might convince me to go along with your plan?"

Since one question after another can feel a lot like an interrogation, use this tool sparingly, preferably interspersing questions among other alignment messages.

Doing Nothing At first, this may seem like a strange alignment tool, but in fact it is an extremely valuable one. There is no rule stating that you must verbally or nonverbally react to a control freak's every move immediately or at all. Saying and doing nothing is itself a response. In fact, when you encounter icy silence, blank stares or pregnant pauses, matching the controller's silence with attentive, receptive silence of your own may be the best option available to you.

"Attentive receptive silence" means signaling with body language and facial expression that you are looking forward to working out the problem when, as, and if the other person chooses. It does *not* mean playing "dueling eyeballs" as you try to stare the other person down. Similarly, don't yawn, check your watch, look bored, hum, or drum your fingers on the tabletop. Instead, relax your body, breathe, maintain good eye-to-face contact, pay careful attention (as always) and wait. How long should you wait before concluding that another tactic is required? That depends on the situation. In general, wait longer than you think you should; you'll be surprised how often your patience will be rewarded.

Get Lots of Practice

Parties, football games, restaurants—you can set up your practice laboratory anywhere. In the case of alignment the problem isn't where to practice, it's where to *start*. There are so many alignment tactics available, and so many ways those tactics can be used, that it can become a bit overwhelming. This chapter alone has mentioned dozens of possibilities, and yet has really only covered a few of the most basic patterns.

One Bite at a Time   That's the best way to eat an elephant, and it is also the best way to learn to align. Pick one specific technique to work on—matching intensity, mirroring movements, paraphrasing. Then, for a day or several days, whenever you come in contact with people, observe, data-collect, and try that technique. Role-play with a friend or relative. Set up a situation and have the other person play the role of the control freak. If they don't know that person themselves, give them enough background information to play their part and ask them to play it to the hilt. Align with the "control freak" until the role player has run out of steam or otherwise finds it difficult to keep up the controlling behavior. Discuss the role play in order to discover what worked and how the other person felt at various points in the dialogue.

If you happen to know someone who has read this book or who is also interested in learning to align, do this practice exercise as we've described it and then switch roles. Or use the modular reprogramming exercises presented in Chapter 6 to learn to align effectively under high-stress conditions.

Anything That's Worth Doing . . .   In *The Amateur*, an espionage novel by Robert Littel published several years ago, the protagonist is asked why he persists in his CIA training. Clearly he is unsuited to the profession—he has no background skills, no aptitude, and makes a fool of himself every time he tries one of the training drills. The young man responds, "To me, it's worth doing. And *anything that's worth doing is worth doing badly.*"

While that philosophy probably doesn't apply so well to

hang gliding or sports car racing, it is absolutely essential for those of us who want to learn more powerful ways to communicate. For most people, learning to align with someone who is acting for all the world like an adversary is not an easy task. It won't feel natural, sometimes it won't even feel right. Furthermore, the first few times you try it you may not meet with much success. The controller will try a move you don't know how to align with, or will upset you so badly you won't be able to align at all.

Don't give up. Hang in there and practice anyway. See the discomfort, the clumsiness, even the doubts you may have as a part of the learning process. Anything that's worth doing is worth doing badly—because that is the only way you'll ever learn to do it well. If you persevere, alignment skills eventually *will* become natural for you, and will serve you in difficult situations for years to come.

167

Alignment is not the end of the road. While the best you can hope for from some control interactions is to ride the tiger and come out alive, in many instances, you will also be able to turn the tiger around, redirecting and guiding it toward a mutually satisfying outcome. The next chapter will explain when and how to do that.

CHAPTER

8

REDIRECTION
How to (Gently) Turn the Tiger Around

"Alignment" is a pretty general term, and it refers to many different skills. But all these skills have at least one thing in common: when wielded successfully, they will all cause the controller to feel attended to, more comfortable, less adversarial, not quite so much alone. Each skill, in some way, addresses a need, and thus leaves the controller feeling just a little less needy.

Further, during this process the controller can continue to do whatever it is she does to control. (The control strategies may not be having exactly the same *effect* they used to, but they still feel like control to the controller, and that's usually good enough.) So her control needs are being served as well. Like the tiger who has eaten recently, the controller whose urge to control has been partially satisfied is less powerfully driven to bully or manipulate. She may not be a pussycat, mind you, but chances are that she has stopped ranting and raving or frantically chipping away at you.

In addition, she may recognize that you aren't responding quite as she would have predicted. You *appear* to be giving in, but not in a way the controller is accustomed to seeing you do it. That puzzles her. Or she expects resistance, encounters none, and is caught off guard. Feeling confused, disarmed, off balance, she pauses to review the situation and reconsider her approach. If you are paying attention, you will know when the "moment of stumble" arrives. This is your opportunity to reach for the reins and gently begin to turn the tiger around.

In this chapter we will explore some redirecting tactics, basic and advanced. They have all been shown to be useful—meaning that they work with some of the people some of the time. Remember, nothing works with everyone, and when you're talking about control freaks you can be sure that with some people, very little works at all. Take your best shot.

Basic Skills

Alignment lays the groundwork for turning the tiger, making whatever you do next more likely to succeed. With that in mind, we'll look at a variety of redirection strategies and effective communication skills, starting with generic tools that can be helpful in many different control situations. The first three tools are the meat and potatoes of good communication.

Metacommunication   169

"Metacommunication" is communication *about the communication currently in process*—the sharing of your insights, thoughts and feelings about that process with the other person or people involved in it. Metacommunication, or metatalk, is an effective way to meet the controller on neutral ground, to move with him into a kind of time-out zone where you can discuss what's going on. Also, it is an excellent *leveling* tactic, as described in Chapter 5.

Metacommunicate by taking the focus off the *content* of your conversation and placing it on the *process* of conversing. Still using information the other person has provided, you might express your feelings about the interaction: "I'm pretty confused about some of the things I'm hearing" or "I don't know about you, but when I get hit with so many ideas at once I feel really overwhelmed. Right now my head is spinning. I'd be able to get a better handle on the problem if we could go over the points one at a time." Here are a few specific ways metacommunication can be used.

Progress Reports   Progress reports help to keep goal-directed communication on track. "It seems like we're going around in circles" or "I think I was more receptive to your ideas before you started yelling at me." Elicit comments on the process from the controller as well: "What do you think? Are we getting any closer to resolving this?" or "I realize you have strong feelings about this matter, so I need to know if there's room for discussion here. Are you willing to hear my point of view?"

Pointing Out Contradictions   You can point out incongruencies, especially those involving nonverbal signals that don't match the other person's words: "I hear you saying that you aren't angry. But when I see you glaring at me, slamming cabinet doors and beating that poor steak into a pulp, I can't help thinking that you really are angry after all." Other examples include: "I know you said you were fine, but that sigh usually means you're upset about something. Do you want to talk about it?" or "Did you mean it when you said you'd hear me out? Because it seems like every time I've started to explain myself, you've interrupted me."

170

Sharing Feelings   Finally, meta-talk gives you a way to let controllers know how their controlling behavior affects you: "When you check up on me, I feel as if you're telling me that I'm incompetent, that you don't trust me to do my job" or "I wish you wouldn't yell. When you do, I get so flustered that I can't think straight. I get tongue-tied. You get impatient and yell some more. It's a vicious cycle."

"When" Statements

"When you do _____, I feel _____."
"When I do/say _____, you seem to _____."

These constructions are called *when statements*. Their value lies in the fact that they do not imply fault, blame or any kind of causal relationship (even though there might be one) between what *you do* and what *I feel*. It's a good idea to use "when" statements in place of statements like "You make me feel _____ when you say/do _____."
Example: "You make me feel angry when you criticize me" becomes "When you criticize me, I feel angry."

Many controllers are oblivious to the impact their actions have on you. When you make them aware of it, they will often change their behavior, at least temporarily.

Of course, some controllers have armor too thick for this technique to penetrate. "Don't psychoanalyze me," they growl when you attempt to metacommunicate. Realign and try again. You just might get through to them. If you don't after several attempts, try something else.

Metacommunicating at the height of a crisis or when you are in a highly emotional state is very difficult to do. If you think it could help, but simply are not calm and composed enough to do it *during* the control interaction, try it at another time. At that later time, introduce the matter by telling the controller you want to discuss your earlier interaction, and if he or she agrees, do so in a non-judgmental, collaborative manner (use when statements).

If a control freak's method for getting you to do things is the primary source of your difficulties, meta-talk may be enough to resolve them. More often, however, metacommunication paves the way for some other form of redirection, or follows up an assertive or easily misinterpreted attempt to get something you want.

Requests

When the energy in the controller's attack has been neutralized, it is time for you to act. Generally, you'll want to make some sort of request. For instance, you can ask that he discontinue certain behaviors: "If you are unhappy with my work, I'd prefer that you tell me about it privately instead of shouting at me in front of the rest of the staff."

You can ask for the controller's cooperation: "I'm really swamped with work this week, Mom. Could you help me out by making a list of wedding details you want me to take care of and reading it to me when I call you at around seven o'clock?" Or for the controller's support: "I know you're not thrilled that I'm taking these night courses, but getting my degree is very important to me. I'd really appreciate it if you would learn my schedule and not make plans for us on the nights I have class."

Or you can take the opportunity to request something the controller has been reluctant to do for you in the past: "I'm glad you brought this up. It gives me a chance to ask you about that raise you mentioned several weeks ago. When will I be getting it?" or "That reminds me, have you gotten the car inspected yet?"

Requests come in two forms: *simple* and *complex.* A simple request is just that, a question or statement that asks for compliance of some kind. "Would you please pass the sugar?" and "I don't want you to ask me out anymore" are simple requests. But there are many, many other ways to make requests. Some of these methods are complex, elegant and extremely subtle. Some can make you crazy—such as the paradoxical request, where the only way to comply is not to comply. Some request tactics align as well as lead—for instance, when you ask for something you know the other person wants to give, in a way that increases your chances that a second, less charitable request will also be granted. In this section we consider the ins and outs of simple requests—and so will only scratch the surface of this fascinating topic.

172

Be Specific When making requests, do not be ambiguous about what you want. Specify exactly what you need to see and hear from the other person—even when you think they should know what you mean. Use clear, concise language that an average ten-year-old could understand. Stay away from vague generalizations about "taking more responsibility around here" or "backing me up when I discipline the kids," or from jargon and street slang that the other person is unlikely to understand. Your artist friend may have no idea how to "interface" and your stockbroker husband may think he is "supporting" you already by bringing home a paycheck.

Be Concise Although softening requests with lead-ins like "Could you help me out by . . ." or "I'd really appreciate it if . . ." can be helpful, try not to weaken your request in the process. When you say, "Could you maybe think about being a little more patient with the kids?" or "It's only a thought and you might not agree with me, but it seems to me that you might get more out of us workers if you just criticized us a little less," you come across as anything *but* committed to your request. As a rule, the less padding you use the better. And once you've made your request, stop talking. If you say nothing else, you'll avoid the common pitfall of providing the controller with information he can use to justify refusing to comply.

If the Controller Resists There are only two possible responses to a request: compliance and resistance. (Of course, there are lots of ways to resist. Also the controller may comply *and* resist.) If the controller explains why she can't possibly help you out, criticizes your position, meets your request with a request of her own (sometimes called "returning the porcupine"), tries to make you feel guilty, gets angry, or does anything besides comply (or agree to comply), align. Use the moves you learned in Chapter 7, one or more of the advanced aikido tactics described later in this chapter, or some other appropriate pattern. Continue to align until you see the stumble, or until the energy in the controller's attack begins to run down. Then repeat your request.

Dealing with Silence Some controllers will greet your request with silence, staring you down in hopes of making you anxious enough to overexplain and minimize your request or rescind it altogether. Or they will ignore you, hoping both you and your request will just go away. Generally, align with silence by being silent back. Maintain good eye contact, breathe, in other words *be present;* just don't say anything.

Most people will yield or switch to another form of resistance when they see their silence tactic isn't going to work. But some will hang tough. So should you. Remember what you learned in Chapter 7: wait longer than you think you should. If the silence becomes unbearable, or if and when it feels strategic to do so, repeat your request in slightly different words, or metacommunicate about the silence. ("Gee, it seems like we've both been staring at each other for a while.") Then be silent once more.

Dealing with Flat or Repeated Refusal Other controllers will flatly refuse to do what you ask. They may interrogate, criticize or ridicule you, go for your guilt button or reach for some other control tactic in order to resist your attempt to get something from them. Realign or metacommunicate (or do both) and then repeat your request, checking to see if they understand what is being asked of them.

If You Can't Get Compliance, Get Acknowledgment If controllers repeatedly refuse, or refuse in a way that creates more discomfort than you can tolerate, ultimately you will hit the point of diminishing returns. Before ending the interaction, try to get them to acknowledge your request—"Do you understand that I'd prefer to be criticized in private rather than being reamed out in front of the staff?" or "Can you hear that I'm asking you not to make plans for us on the nights I have classes?" When you get a yes, acknowledge it ("Thank you for hearing me out") and leave it at that. If the yes is followed by a "but," interrupt and acknowledge the yes.

Warmly Acknowledge *Any* Compliance   Whenever a controller *does* agree to grant your request, warmly acknowledge that agreement. Hand out a few positive strokes, complimenting the controller for being reasonable, flexible, understanding, willing to take chances or anything else that applies. You need not be effusive. But *do not* sound sarcastic.

Dealing with a Mixed Bag   What about the controller with an attitude? You ask your teenager, Chucky, to clean up the milk he spilt, and Chucky does so—grumbling and slamming drawers—after giving you a look that would put Medusa to shame. What do you do? You thank him for doing what you asked. No matter that he grumbled doing it. No matter that he should have volunteered to clean it up. *Whenever* your request is complied with, you reward that compliance and finish the interaction with acknowledgment.

If you would like to talk to Chucky about his attitude, fine. Actually, that sounds like a good idea. But do it in a "new paragraph"—that is, finish acknowledging the cleanup, stop, take a breath or two. If you can stand it, wait a few minutes. Then, as a brand-new topic, sit down with Chucky and pop the subject of attitude. (Good luck.)

Dealing with Agreement Followed by Noncompliance   Chucky agrees to clean up his room (his sloppiness extends beyond the breakfast table); next thing you know, Xaxxon warriors are charging into your living room from the Nintendo machine. The trick here is repetition. Don't get angry (if you can help it); you don't have to say it louder or better. Just say it again. "Go clean up your room."

Using Consequences   An employee gets censured or fired if she is repeatedly late for work. A child who comes home two hours late gets grounded, or loses his TV privileges or his allow-

174

ance. A friend who betrays a confidence winds up with a hurt and angry friend.

It's *fine* to use consequences. I suggest you don't "lead" with consequences, except as a last resort or when you can't do anything else. Generally, use positive as well as negative consequences; for example, let Chucky know what favor, privilege or reward he will get if he *does* clean his room. Don't threaten with consequences: they should be given even to young children as *choices,* not ultimatums. "Get to bed by eight-thirty, I'll read you a story. Miss your bedtime, no TV tomorrow night. Got that?" (Of course, if your kids routinely choose the negative consequence, your consequences are too soft—it's time to up the ante.)

I believe immediate, negative consequences should follow whenever someone agrees to comply with your request and then fails to do so. A child should be punished, an employee censured, a friend confronted. Let the people around you know that you see *agreeing to comply* as virtually synonymous with actually complying, and you expect them to act accordingly. Of course, you should do the same. Among other things, once you set the conditions for a consequence (positive or negative), *never* fail to follow through if those conditions are satisfied. It only takes a few "hollow consequences" to ruin your credibility and put a real crimp in your ability to get any compliance at all.

175

Refusals

If you find it difficult to picture yourself making requests, and the controllers in your life agree to fulfill them, you will probably find it impossible to imagine refusing to comply with the control freak's demands. Most of us have a hard time saying no, and even more so when the other person is unwilling to take no for an answer. But it can be done.

Assess the Situation   First, realistically assess your situation. Are there circumstances which make saying no a greater risk than you want to take? Could you lose your job? Get arrested? Would you put another person in danger? Is there a distinct possibility that the person you refuse would become violent? If such consequences could actually occur, then refusal probably is not an option—no matter how much you wish it could be.

Costs and Benefits Would you feel guilty? Worry about getting paid back at a later date? Have to put up with an angry tirade, a long-winded debate, a litany of reminders about all the things the other person has done for you? If so, you must weigh those unpleasant repercussions against your needs or goals, and decide if refusal is an option you are willing to pursue.

What's In It for You Finally, honestly appraise your motives. Do you resent the request or how it was made? Are you still angry about something the controller said or did earlier in the interaction or at another time? Has it crossed your mind that by resisting now you would get even for what he did previously? If those or other vindictive motives are present, mentally step back, center yourself and reexamine the demand or request. You may discover that you are willing and able to comply with *part* of the controller's plan or that you could go along with him if he modified his demand in some way. If that is the case, try a redirection strategy or communication tool other than refusal.

Don't Wobble There is an ancient Japanese saying that roughly translates to "When you sit, sit. When you stand, stand. Don't wobble." If you do decide that you absolutely do *not* want to do what the controller is asking of you and that there is absolutely *no* room for compromise, then you must say so. Say it firmly, say it gently, say it regretfully, say it in a way that causes the least amount of pain, embarrassment, or loss of face—but say it.

Sometimes it's useful to paraphrase the request or demand. Verify both to yourself and to the controller that you understand what is being asked. Then deliver your no. If you've decided to be firm, declare, "I am unwilling to do that." Or say, "I understand that you want me to give up my night courses [call the caterer right away/tell you what Joe is doing with the Widget account/go out with you], but I won't [or I'd prefer not to]."

White Lies There is nothing wrong with white lies. Exaggerated or fabricated reasons for saying no, excuses (including that most generic of excuses, "I can't"), all of these have their place. If everyone were totally honest and revealing with everyone else on the planet, we'd kill one another off inside of a year. But the *motive* for lying is important. A white lie is told to avoid hurting someone else. If you're lying because you're too embarrassed to tell the truth, or for some other self-serving reason you're not using the aikido model. And you probably are creating trouble for yourself somewhere down the road.

Agreeing to Disagree A negotiation tactic for use when the other person is unwilling to take no for an answer goes like this:

JANE: *(After several rounds of arguing)* For the last time, we have to bid this contract—we can't afford not to.
YOU: I don't think so, I think we should pass it up.
JANE: That's crazy, we have the manpower, and we need the money.
YOU: Jane, I think we have a difference of opinion about this.
JANE: Yeah, the difference is I'm right and you're crazy!
YOU: Well, I think we have a difference of opinion there, too.

177

Jane certainly can't argue about that—it's obviously true. "Agreeing to disagree" is a tactic intended to table unresolvable issues for later. It is saved for use as a last resort, after alignment and other approaches have been attempted. Ideally, the parties work together to define what similarities and differences are in their positions and at least agree on that. If appropriate, you can soften the fact that you initiated agreeing to disagree by saying something like, "Maybe I'll feel differently about this in the morning" or "I need some time to think about it."

Dealing with Resistance Be prepared for resistance. As you well know, you are dealing with someone who hates to be turned down (and has little practice taking no's gracefully). Thwarted controllers will do anything from throwing tantrums to accusing you of high treason in order to change your mind. Be a broken record. Realign, repeat their request, and paraphrase any new twists they've added. Then repeat your refusal. Remember that most no's are for now, not forever. Remain open to the messages the controllers are conveying. If they actually show you a reason for doing things their way which makes sense to you and convinces you that it would not cost you much to comply, then by all means do so.

If You Can't Stand the Heat . . . Unfortunately, there are times when the controller will not only refuse to take no for an answer, but will continue to browbeat you until the costs of refusing have begun to substantially outweigh the benefits. If this ever happens to you, if you simply can't tolerate the flak you're getting for refusing, give yourself a break. It's okay to yield in the interest of survival. Bow out of *this* battle as gracefully as you can, in order to be around long enough to eventually win the war.

However, do work on your ability to stand up for yourself. When you say no and then back down later, you are showing control freaks that their tactics work on you. Next time they'll try even longer and harder to change your mind. So unless you're willing to disconnect from them forever (a choice you might consider!), rehearse, reprogram and build up your resources against the day when you'll have the power to take a carefully considered position and not back down.

178

Limit-Setting

Limit-setting is really a hybrid skill—look closely and you'll see a combination of the three previous tactics: metacommunicating, requesting, and refusing. However, the outcome it can achieve (relative freedom from the demands of the control freak) is so important that I teach it as a separate skill.

In its simplest form, limit-setting simply means communicating your boundaries, your "non-negotiables" to the controller. The limit-setter essentially says, "Up to this point, X happens. Beyond this point, Y happens." People set limits all the time without even realizing they're doing it. Often it can be done while maintaining close rapport—properly framed, the other person may actually hear your limit as an opportunity, or a compliment.

THE DESC MODEL

DESC is an acronym that stands for Describe, Express, Specify [and Share] Consequences. It is a general assertion skill that lends itself well to high-pressure limit-setting. The four component steps can be performed separately (eliciting and aligning with the controller's response between each) or together, as a unit.

DESCRIBE:	Clearly describe the behavioral pattern you want to eliminate or limit, and your reactions to it.
EXPRESS:	Succinctly but firmly describe how you feel about the target behavior.
SPECIFY:	Tell the controller precisely what limits you want to set, or what you want to see change.
CONSEQUENCE:	Tell the controller exactly what will happen if he doesn't comply with this request. (Optional but recommended: Also tell him what positive consequences will occur if he cooperates.)

But when you hang around a control freak, limit-setting is sometimes a bit more difficult. The controller doesn't want limits. You're afraid to set them. Or you set them, the controller ignores them, and you're afraid to enforce the consequences. For people who have trouble limit-setting, we borrow from the work of Sharon Bower, a management consultant and, with her husband, author of the excellent book on assertive communication *Asserting Yourself: A Practical Guide for Positive Change.* She calls her approach the DESC model (see box).

DESC is a four-step communication strategy which, in combination with other social skills, can be useful in a variety of interpersonal situations. But the DESC model can also be practiced and applied alone, as a kind of generic communication script. In this form it is particularly easy to remember and use under pressure, and thus can be a valuable limit-setting tool.

A word of caution here. When used in bare-bones form, as is done in the following example, DESC is emphatically *not* an alignment strategy. You describe the situation, say how you feel about it, state what you want, and tell the other person what will happen if he or she doesn't comply. That's it. Someone using bare-bones DESC can come across as heavy-handed, insensitive, and inflexible—the technique should be used in this form only as a last resort!

Still, many accommodators who have spent years being abused by control freaks just aren't up to the alignment stage yet. When the controller moves in, they can barely remember how to talk, let alone paraphrase or match intensity. Their very survival is on the line: they *need* last resorts. For them, DESC can be a godsend.

DESC in Action   Betty is badly intimidated by Roger, her supervisor. At the weekly team meeting, Roger is often critical of Betty's work, and sometimes stoops to ridicule. But frightened or not, Betty has had it, and now, finally, she has a way to do something about it. She begins by identifying the inappropriate behavior, couching her delivery in a "when" statement. Then she goes right through the four steps without allowing Roger to interrupt her. (She knows that if she gets sidetracked she'll probably never finish, and will feel as if she's chickened out again.) She speaks to Roger one on one if possible; but if pushed or as a last resort she DESC's him right at the staff meeting.

BETTY: Roger, I want to talk to you, please.

ROGER: Sure, what about?

BETTY: About how you treated me in staff this morning. When you ridicule me in front of the staff like that, I get upset and very angry! I also can't focus on the meeting anymore *(D)*.

ROGER: I didn't—

BETTY: Roger, please let me finish. I don't like you treating me that way. I think it's unfair and I'm not going to stand for it *(E)*. *I want you to stop (S).* If you don't stop . . . well, I don't know what I'll do. But I'm not going to let it drop *(C)*.

ROGER: I'm amazed! When did you get the idea I was ridiculing you? I—

BETTY: Roger, I'm sorry, that's how I see it. Whatever you call it, please stop, okay?

In a perfect world, Betty would be able to confront Roger in a relaxed confident manner, using rapport and alignment skills, letting Roger have his say, clarifying his position, and so on. But she simply can't do that. So for the time being she settles for basic limit-setting. Later, she can begin to work toward reducing some of her automatic reactions and developing more advanced skills.

Advanced Tactics

The manner in which this book is laid out suggests that align-ment and redirecting are done in sequence—that is, first you align, then you redirect. In fact, this is true only in a limited sense. In fact, at more advanced levels it is often difficult to tell an alignment strategy from a redirection strategy, because most techniques have both an alignment component and a redirection component built into them. So, while we distinguish between these stages for training purposes, often that distinction is more theoretical than real.

Also, many advanced tactics are not entirely direct. In truth, any tactic that doesn't actually harm someone can be a valuable aikido move. For instance, some of the emotional hooks listed in Chapter 7 also have useful, ethical applications. Hypnotists use forced-choice tactics and presuppositions to induce healing trances; guests use deception to help their hostess feel better about a meal that didn't turn out very well, and so on. There is nothing wrong with indirect or complex communication, as long as it is used with the intent to serve and collaborate, rather than to manipulate and control.

At this level, everything really boils down to your intention and the results you get. If you *mean* to collaborate, and if you *succeed* in collaborating, generally it isn't so important what you did to get there. At times, very indirect, "manipulative" tactics can serve the other person's needs much more effectively than a more "honest," direct approach. Similarly, direct, honest communication can be used to hurt, control, and abuse. Com-munication tactics simply are tools, after all. A hammer can be used to build or destroy—it all depends on what you do with it. Don't avoid indirect tactics just because they're indirect. How-ever, do make sure you use them with integrity.

That said, here are a few more advanced procedures to use in conjunction with the aikido alternative.

Qualified Agreement ("You Might Be Right")

When a control freak believes she is right and you are wrong, or when she's angry about some real or imagined slight, she is often very difficult to deal with. Your first job is to get into alignment with her, establish rapport. Then, maybe you'll have a chance to sort things out. That's where qualified agreement comes in: respond to the controller's outburst by acknowledging that she *might be right.* Then ask specific questions to get more information.

JANET: How the hell could you write a funding proposal like this? We couldn't get Monopoly money with this thing!

PETER: *(Matching Janet's intensity without sounding angry)* You may have a point. Specifically where do you think the problems are with it?

It's okay to say "You may be right," even when you're pretty sure the controller is wrong. Remember, you're only giving *qualified* agreement; if necessary, you can reassess later on. (On the other hand, when the other person *is* right, by all means say so without qualification.) At this point in the encounter, most angry, righteous controllers badly need that "concession" in order to begin to lighten up themselves. You can afford to give it to them, in the interest of alignment. Besides, who knows, they really might be right.

Qualified agreement is a particularly useful tool for dealing with explosive anger. Remember to follow it up with a specific, issue-focused question or statement, to redirect the controller's attention away from you and back onto the subject at hand. Continue to align; but if you feel you need to, begin looking for the first opportunity to disconnect.

By the way, no one has the right to speak to you the way Janet spoke to Peter. If you want to make a request ("Please don't talk to me that way"), metacommunicate ("I don't like it when you talk to me that way"), limit-set ("Chill out or I'm leaving!"), or simply walk away, that's fine. Qualified agreement provides another useful option—you choose which one you think will work best for you.

Decoding

There are a lot of ways to decode. They all involve responding to what you think is the sender's *intent,* rather than to what he or she actually says. Here are some times when it might be useful to decode.

Differences of Opinion   One of the simplest, most common forms of decoding is the paraphrase in which you "lead" the other person to the heart of the matter under discussion. To use it, *tentatively* interpret messages you are receiving rather than (or in addition to) simply paraphrasing them. This leeway enables you to confront hidden agendas and unspoken implications and perhaps get the controller to acknowledge them. One caution: remember to frame your responses as tentative hypotheses rather than as statements of fact. The idea is to help the other person talk about a problem or issue—not accuse him of having one! Your comments should not convey the message "Aha! *I* know what you're thinking!" but rather, "I think this may be going on with you, and if it is, I'd be glad to talk about it."

In the following example, a mother uses leading paraphrase with her teenage daughter:

TEEN: Carrie's mother lets her take the train into the city by herself.

MOM: I guess you wish I was more like Carrie's mom.

TEEN: I just wish you'd let me take the train into the city so I could go to the concert with Carrie. Even *you* should know teenagers do that today and live to tell about it.

MOM: Sounds like you think I'm too old-fashioned and overprotective.

This conversation ended with the teen having a better understanding of the mother's position and the mother agreeing to drive her daughter to a different concert, one being held closer to home the following week. Now consider how the interaction might have proceeded if Mom had fought back instead:

TEEN: Carrie's mother lets her take the train into the city by herself.

MOM: I'm *not* Carrie's mother and if you're going to start bugging me about that stupid concert, you can save your breath. I told you that you couldn't go and I meant it.

TEEN: It's *not* a *stupid* concert. You don't understand anything!

MOM: I understand that no daughter of mine is going to dress

TEEN: like a groupie and go to a concert in a city full of muggers and drug addicts.

TEEN: Oh please! You don't have a clue. You're living in a time warp. You think you're June Cleaver or something. Well, you're not. You're a . . .

You get the idea.

Blowing Off Steam Sometimes aggression, criticism, anger, or one of the emotional hooks described in Chapter 7 can serve as a kind of code, can mean something that really has little to do with attack or emotional exploitation. For instance, Dudley is watching TV when his wife, Teresa, comes home from the office. In the hall, she trips over their three-year-old's rattle and nearly falls. Clearly this is the last straw for Teresa.

"Bleep!" she yells. "Dudley, if you gave a bleep about me or this house you'd bleeping clean up *before sitting down to watch TV.* And she slams upstairs. Now, Dudley doesn't particularly like being yelled at, or being sworn at, and in fact makes a mental note to bring up the issue (metacommunicate) with Teresa after she's calmed down. On the other hand, he doesn't take it personally, because he can easily *decode* her words and actions: Teresa always has been a bit volatile, and she clearly has had a bad day. Her energy and unpredictability are among the things he loves about her most, and he is willing to accept the bad with the good. Furthermore, he knows she'll be down in half an hour with a kiss and a story about something crazy that happened at the office. So he shrugs and changes the channel. (At some point he may also go over and pick up the rattle.)

Embedded Message as Polite Behavior Sometimes what sounds like a hook isn't a hook at all, but simply the sender's way of being polite, or of softening criticism or a request. In these cases, decode the request or statement, rather than demanding that the sender adhere to the letter of "good" communication.

Here is a personal example. My mother used to phrase requests (which ultimately, of course, I could not refuse) in the form of questions. Lots of people do that; it's an accepted form of polite communication. For instance, Mom would ask, "Gerry, would you like to take the garbage out now?"

Under some circumstances this question can be manipula-

184

tive, but my mother was just trying to be nice, and everybody in the room knew it. However, I was going through my "communication expert" phase and wasn't going to let her get away with embedding a request in a question! So I would answer in a pleasant, friendly tone, "No, Mom. I don't think I'd like that." (Translation: "I'll take out the garbage, but only if you ask me *my* way.") My mother's face would fall, and everyone else in the room would look at me as if I were a Martian.

It is amazing how obnoxious and counterproductive "good communication" can be when it's applied arbitrarily or automatically, without regard for people and their feelings. I should have read the *intent* behind my mother's words, responded to the request rather than the question, and taken out the garbage. I wasn't being a good communicator, and I wasn't being a Martian —I was just being a pain.

Of course, in order to decode, you need to know the code. If it turns out the sender *is* trying to manipulate you after all, you'll probably get hooked. But when you can, assume the sender is being straight with you for the first couple of rounds. Pay attention, and see what happens. If you get hooked? Well, now you know; lick your wounds and change your response. A bit of folk wisdom applies here: "Fool me once, shame on you. Fool me twice, shame on me."

185

When Not to Decode   On the other hand, when you're pretty sure the other person is really trying to manipulate or attack you, it may be most effective *not* to decode. Many years ago I was conducting an assertion training workshop for a large group of professionals at a national conference. It was my first-ever "major" presentation, and I was pretty nervous about it.

Things were going reasonably smoothly when, about midway through the first morning, a woman in back stood up. She waved her sheaf of seminar handouts at me and shouted, "May I ask a question?"

"Sure."

"Does the fact that you've used mostly male examples, both in your handouts and in your talk," she asked, her voice dripping sarcasm and contempt, "mean that you're a male chauvinist pig with absolutely no sensitivity for women's issues in this country?"

Two hundred people went absolutely silent: you could hear a pin drop. It was clearly my move. What in God's name should I say? I thought of using an agreement or paraphrase tactic to defuse her obvious trap question, saying something like "I'm hearing you say you'd like me to use more women in my handouts and examples . . ." but somehow I sensed they'd be picking me up with a sponge if I tried anything like that. Besides, right or wrong, here I was being ferociously attacked in front of two hundred people at an assertion training seminar! I had the audience's needs (and my own) to think about as well as those of the speaker. So I decided to parry the attack and see what happened.

I walked toward the front of the stage and, turning my head for a moment to include the entire audience, I metacommented in a level tone *without the slightest bit of sarcasm,* "Okay. Now, I'm going to answer that as if it were a straight question."

I turned back to the questioner. Keeping my intensity up, but in as pleasant and neutral a tone of voice as I could muster (sounding angry *at all* would have been disastrous), I said, "No." Then I just waited, open body posture, eyes on the questioner.

The woman's mouth opened, but obviously she couldn't think of anything to say (the "moment of stumble"). The dead, ominous silence went on for hours (actually about three seconds). Then the tension broke; the audience laughed, I think as much in relief as anything else.

But the woman in the back held her ground. "What *does* it mean, then?" she said angrily.

"I think it shows an oversight on my part," I answered. "I think you're right, I should use more female examples. This is an important issue, and I thank you for bringing it to my attention." The woman sat down.

Tactically, I deflected the woman's attack by *answering her loaded question literally,* rather than decoding it and responding to the obvious embedded meaning. This is a variation of a technique I learned a long time ago from psychologist Errol Schubot, who called it "flushing." We'll take another look at the flushing technique later in the chapter.

One final comment. The questioner clearly had a good point about my examples and handouts, and in fact the feedback she gave me helped me align more effectively with female participants in future seminars. So, why did I flush her? First, because there was a big problem with the *way* she made her point. People assault you with the truth all the time; sometimes it's important to neutralize the assault before you acknowledge the validity of the point they want to make. Second, although her observations were technically correct, the *conclusions* she drew from those observations were not, and I wanted to make that clear.

Shading

"Shading" is the prototypical advanced verbal aikido skill. In most variations, a combination of paraphrase, suggestion and assumption are used to lead the conversation in a productive direction or maximize the chances for agreement. There are many, many ways to shade; here are a few examples.

Assumed Agreement Assuming the other person will agree with you keeps the atmosphere positive and usually keeps energy moving in the right direction. However, a delicate touch is required: assume too much and he or she will feel short-circuited, and may begin to resist on general principles.

187

There is a specific variation on assumed agreement tailor-made for people who short-circuit you by missing deadlines, not returning phone calls, and so on. Let's say you want a written agreement from Martha on a particular contract modification which you must present to the contractor by Friday. You send her your proposal a week early, get no reply, call, get no response, and now it's Wednesday. Send Martha a *traceable* memo or E-mail message (with copies to your and/or her boss if appropriate at your company) saying, in part, "I know you're busy, and you may like the contract the way it is. So, unless I receive your proposed contract changes by Thursday noon, I'll assume you approve the current version and will work up a presentation as we discussed."

This kind of memo may not be legally binding, but it certainly isn't going to hurt you any. In my experience, people who send this kind of memo get more cooperation from their colleagues than people who don't. They also tend to get their phone calls returned.

Selective Responding A common control tactic involves mixing positives and negatives in the same message (for instance, embedding a criticism in a compliment so it is harder to deflect). One way to respond to this ploy is to select out the positive part of the message and respond only to it. Temporarily ignore the negative part, and see what happens. If it comes up again later in the conversation, you'll have to deal with it; but if it doesn't, you can forget about it or bring it up at a time when it can be dealt with productively (when the other person is less upset, when you have more time or more privacy, and so on). Alternatively, respond to the positive part first, then just touch on the negative component to see if the controller wants to take it further.

JOAN: You're always late for lunch . . . you never call me any more . . . God, we used to be good friends, but now you treat me like garbage!

FRAN: You're right, Joan. We've been very good friends. And for a long time. *(Waits for a response.)* [Optional: Do you really think that's changed?]

188

Direction Shifts Nearly any preference or point of view can be expressed in either positive or negative form. For example, my son Ryan might tell me how he'd like to spend his Thursday evening by saying either "I don't want to go to karate practice tonight," or "I'd like to join the rest of the kids for pizza." A powerful redirection tactic can involve shifting the form of the speaker's statement from negative to positive, or vice versa. Often the key to the success of this tactic is in the specific form of paraphrase used. Direction shifting is a complex tactic and is usually used in conjunction with other moves. Here is a simple example.

SALLY: *(Angrily)* Give up, Janice! We'll never sell this plan to Richard. He's a real bear when it comes to changing contractors in midproject!

JANICE: *(Intensely)* Wow, I didn't realize it would be that bad! It sounds like if we're going to have any chance at all, we're really going to have to do our homework.

SALLY: *That's* for sure. It would take a lot of convincing.

JANICE: Might even be worth having an extra meeting before we pitch him, make sure we cover every possibility . . .

SALLY: Well, I suppose we could make some new slides . . .

Please be sure you understand this example; it illustrates an extremely powerful tactic. Janice paraphrased "We'll never sell this plan . . ." as "If we're going to have any chance at all . . ." She used a leading paraphrase, but she also shifted the *direction of movement* implied by Sally's words from negative ("no chance," "give up") to positive ("any chance," "do our homework"). In addition, she used presuppositions—for instance, before we pitch him" implies that Janice and Sally have already agreed to pitch him).

Anticipation Tactics

"Anticipation tactics" involve beating the controller to the punch in one way or another. Let's say your associate is upset because your part of the project is lagging behind schedule, and is probably going to discuss the problem in staff meeting. Go to his office and bring it up first. In that way, you pick the venue and the time—who knows, you may be able to settle the issue one on one, without having to spread it all over the department. Also, for various reasons, you generally will appear more confident and your position will appear somewhat stronger if you initiate the interaction.

189

There are a lot of variations on this theme. If your boss is going to assign you a project, and you can see no way out, don't just sit there waiting for a miracle. Volunteer for the project before she assigns it to you. If you know your mother is going to ask you to get her a 7-Up from the kitchen, ask her first if she'd like something cold to drink. You'll get more points, and believe it or not, in the long run may even save yourself some trips to the kitchen.

Verbal anticipation tactics sometimes involve finishing people's sentences for them. Rather than paraphrasing what the other person just said, you paraphrase what you think he is about to say. Sounds obnoxious, but when done properly it is one of the most powerful redirection strategies around. This is partly because it can be combined so easily with other patterns, such as shading and leading paraphrase. Good hosts, politicians, salespeople and business executives do this so skillfully you barely realize it's happening. Mainly you feel the other person is in very close rapport, really understands you, that your two minds are functioning almost as one. Of course, the strategic anticipator doesn't just finish your sentences—she finishes them in a way that delicately steers the conversation in a direction she would like it to go.

Whatever Works

A tremendous number of advanced alignment tactics are available. In truth, any tactic that *fills the other person's need* in some way can be an alignment/redirection device. This opens up a lot of possibilities for people who have learned to pay attention well enough. Theoretically, it ought to be possible to align with *anything,* and then redirect accordingly. However, at this level of sophistication, alignment can look pretty strange—sometimes it can look like anything but alignment.

Let's say my wife comes home from work one evening, puts down her briefcase, and calls out, "Hi, Gerry."

"Grumph!" comes the response from the living room. Joan walks in and sees her husband sprawled out in front of "Monday Night Football," a Coke in his hand and his shod feet on the new couch. This doesn't make Joan very happy, but she can handle it.

"Who's winning?" asks Joan.

"Who cares?" growls the thing on the couch. "The computer went down today and I lost half a chapter. What's for dinner, anyway?"

At this point, Joan pauses to take stock. She knows her husband very well, she can empathize, she can metacommunicate, and she can paraphrase so well it doesn't even sound like a technique. But she can also observe and decode. Gerry's clearly had a bad day; he looks and acts as if he needs to go out and kill something.

It crosses Joan's mind to sit next to her husband, hold his hand and say, "Gee, I'll bet you've had one rotten day. Want to tell me about it?" Or, "Gee, I'll bet you've had one rotten day. But I still get upset when you snap at me. Can you understand that?" These would both be reasonable alternatives, and either might work (or might lose her a finger). But in this instance, Joan senses that neither would touch what's really going on, and actually might make things worse. Something else is called for.

"I think," says Joan to herself, "Gerry needs a fight. Come to think of it, I could use one myself."

So Joan walks around the coffee table and says, "Forget dinner. Get your shoes off the new couch!"

"What??"

"And for that matter, why the hell didn't you back up your chapter? You're always telling *me* to back up *my* work."

Battle Royal! But both parties are reasonably clean fighters, and neither has much old resentment stored up; so after about fifteen minutes things are calm again. Calm and different! Joan's husband has turned back into Dr. Jekyll: he's smiling, talking—he even volunteered to go pick up the kids.

Gerry has been thoroughly aligned with; and the alignment tactic used was a *real fight.* Please be clear on that—Joan chose to fight in order to align. But in no way did she *fake* the fight. She just chose to air her grievances then rather than at some other time, and she aired them in a somewhat less delicate manner than she otherwise might have done.

Let me reemphasize something else. With many people, Joan's tactic would not have been an ideal, or even a constructive, way to respond. I've shown drafts of this chapter to people who looked at me a little strangely and said, "Uh, that's nice, but I think I'd rather my wife understand I've had a bad day and just be honest with me." Generally, so would I. There is no question that honesty and understanding are important parts of any successful marriage. But with some people and under certain circumstances, other alternatives (humor, a pep talk—or even a fight) might work even better.

191

Note: This is a very advanced, very tricky maneuver. Please be careful with it. Do not attempt it unless you know exactly what you are doing, know your partner and his or her reaction patterns intimately, and are willing to suffer the consequences if the whole thing blows up in your face.

General Communication Guidelines

• *Be specific:* Talk about actual behaviors and specific incidents. Stay away from global accusations ("You *always* want it your way" or "You *never* listen to a word I say").

• *Use "I" statements and "when" statements:* Focus on yourself—your feelings and beliefs when making requests or observations—rather than on the controller. "When you break your promises, I feel frustrated" rather than "You frustrate me by being so undependable." Or "I'd like to have some say in this decision" rather than "You should consult me before you make decisions for both of us."

• *Be polite:* Treat the controller with the same respect you would offer any fellow human being. Avoid name-calling, hitting below the belt, bringing up sore subjects. Address behavior, not personality traits.

• *Don't hit and run:* Don't make your move when the controller is on her way out the door, or trying to concentrate on something else; avoid starting discussions five minutes before a client is due to meet with you, or in the car on the way to a party.

• *Keep calm:* If things start to heat up, take time out to cool off or break the tension with a bit of humor or some positive process talk such as "This is really difficult, but I know we can get through it." Recognize that you do not have to *feel* a certain way in order to *act* a certain way. Acknowledge emotions that you normally give in to, set them aside, and use centering techniques to keep you on track.

• *Stay flexible:* Stick to your bottom line, but leave everything else open to negotiation.

• *Reward all positives:* Mention any and all signs of flexibility, sensitivity, willingness to compromise, and so on. Give progress reports at various points in the interaction, letting the controller know what you feel good about or find reassuring. Even if you make no headway whatsoever, thank the controller for taking the time to discuss the matter with you.

192

Negotiation and Compromise

Negotiation and compromise involve clarifying your own and the controller's needs or goals and hammering out a deal that allows both of you to get at least some of what you want. Because the controlling people in your life generally want the whole pie and look at compromises in terms of what they lost rather than what they gained, they will be receptive to this option only if you have successfully aligned with them and led them to believe that taking half or three quarters of the pie might actually be in their best interest.

Don't try to negotiate with someone who is still obviously in control mode and don't even mention the word "compromise" to anyone who is still yelling, making threats, sending double messages or giving you the silent treatment. Even after the other person seems to have settled down and accepted your subtler efforts to redirect him, be prepared for a negative reaction to the idea of negotiation and compromise. Realign. Metacommunicate. Use whatever advanced tactics you think might be appropriate. And once the controller agrees to at least try to cut a deal, if tension remains in the air, arrange to negotiate at another, mutually agreeable time.

To negotiate effectively:

193

1. Specify that your goal is to come up with an *imperfect* solution. Agree to do your best to come up with the alternative that allows each of you to obtain the most benefits at the lowest possible cost.

2. Establish a few essential ground rules. These might include no yelling, name calling or "kitchen sinking" (bringing up issues that are not related to the specific conflict you are working to resolve). A rule that prohibits walking away from the bargaining table without setting a date for negotiations to resume is particularly useful. If you get bogged down at this stage, one of you is not really ready to negotiate. Realign. Redirect. Or try again at another time.

3. Define the issue. Paraphrase and use specificity questions to make sure that both of you understand what the problem is as well as each other's thoughts and feelings about it.

4. Propose possible solutions. In addition to your individual best possible outcomes and bottom lines (the least you are willing to accept), brainstorm as many other options as possible. Don't judge them yet. Just propose them. The more options the better—even if some of them seem pretty weird at first glance.

5. Talk about the costs and benefits of various solutions. Combine options if you'd like. Agree on one that both of you are willing to accept. Make a *time-limited* commitment to that option. Consider it an experiment and set a date to evaluate the results.

6. Implement the agreed-upon course of action and use re-alignment or other redirection strategies to point out violations. (You can expect some from a dyed-in-the-wool control freak.)

7. Evaluate the outcome on the agreed-upon date and decide whether you will renew your agreement or renegotiate it.

Be aware that some controllers will simply refuse to negotiate and that some will readily agree to compromise but then do whatever they darn well please. Take your best shot at making this strategy work, but if it doesn't, don't beat a dead horse. Try something else instead.

Specialty Tactics

Here are five additional tactics for use in specific types of situations, or when dealing with specific controllers. Some of them are advanced and require good timing, alignment skills, and so on. Others are more straightforward. They involve knowing what to do rather than how to do it. As always, begin with the basics—collect data and successfully align with the controller before making your move.

The Two-Hat Technique

This is an important technique to have available. We have all experienced multiple-role relationships at one time or another; most of us have several going on at once. Many managers become good friends with their supervisees. My children's mother is also my wife, business partner, friend and lover (and sparring partner). My son's father is also his soccer coach.

There is nothing intrinsically wrong with two- (or multiple-) role relationships, but they can get complicated. Under certain circumstances the roles you play (the "hats" you wear) may begin to conflict with one another. What do you do then?

I tell trainees that, as far as their hats are concerned, they should act as if they *really are two people.* They should separate their roles completely, and then deal independently with the responsibilities of each.

For instance, Bob, the marketing director for a large software company, was told by his very aggressive, very controlling boss, Marge, that marketing plans for a certain new product were being changed. Now, Marge was CEO and ultimately called the shots. But new-product marketing was normally under Bob's authority; as an expert with a proven track record, he was the person best equipped to make these kinds of decisions. Evidently, Marge was up to her old tricks again: she would delegate authority, and then when she got nervous at the last minute, she would take it back and act unilaterally. More to the point, Bob was pretty sure Marge's decision was wrong.

Bob had a two-hat problem. In this case the roles causing the conflict were *employee* (employees get paid to do what they're told) and *expert* (experts get paid a premium wage to have specialized knowledge and to make decisions based on that knowledge). If Bob used his expert knowledge, he'd be going against a directive from his boss. If he did what she told him to do, he'd feel he wasn't doing the best possible job (and, as marketing was his responsibility, he knew it would come back to haunt him later on). Here is how Bob applied the two-hat technique by *sequentially* playing the roles of employee and expert.

The day after receiving her directive, Bob asked Marge for a few minutes of her time. In a calm, confident manner he said, "I'd like about five minutes to play marketing consultant. You pay me good money because I know that area; and I think I have information you need to know in order to make the best decision about our new product. Anyway, give me five minutes. Then I'll put my employee hat back on, you tell me what you want done, and I'll do it to the best of my ability. Okay?"

Marge agreed, so Bob went on to give his viewpoint clearly and decisively (like an expert). He laid out the issues as he saw them, and then answered the questions Marge asked. Then he relaxed, and said, "Okay, thanks for listening to my opinion. Now it's your call. Let me know what you want me to do, and I'll get started."

Bob may or may not get his way, as far as the marketing plans are concerned, but he felt he took his best shot. Further, by using the two-hat technique, he was able to get out of an uncomfortable situation. As employee, he avoided disobeying his boss; and as expert, he got his opinion heard. Finally, he was able to deal with Marge in a way she could see as neither insubordinate nor weak. Marge might not have liked what Bob told her, but the chances are she will respect him for the manner in which he was able to say it.

The "I've Got a Problem" Technique

When negative consequences (an angry tirade, criticism, the silent treatment) seem to loom on the horizon, you can solicit the intimidator's assistance, literally asking him how to approach the situation without suffering those consequences.

Sam encountered numerous problems while on the assignment Cassie had bullied him into accepting. He knew that he needed to bring those problems to Cassie's attention, but each time he thought about doing so, he imagined her sitting at her cluttered desk, shouting orders at her harried staff and being annoyed by the mere fact that he was there. Even though he was convinced that he would once again be verbally assaulted, Sam resisted the temptation to handle matters himself and went in to see Cassie.

"I have a problem," he said firmly, maintaining good eye contact. "I need to tell you about a concern I have about the project. But I know you have a lot going on, and I have no desire to get you angry. What's the best way for me to bring this to your attention?"

Obviously, Sam had *already* brought the matter to Cassie's attention. But in addition he'd embedded his request in an anticipation tactic that communicated a very real concern. And Cassie got the message. She knew she overreacted from time to time, and she was aware of the bind that she sometimes created for her contractors by doing so. A part of her was embarrassed by her temper (although another part reveled in the power it gave her), and she would certainly never have brought it up herself. But she got kind of a kick out of the solution Sam had come up with. He was asking *Cassie* how to deal with *Cassie*. It actually made sense, when she thought about it.

"Uh, I think you'd better sit down and tell me about the problem," she said with a slight smile. Sam did so, and though he was in fact the bearer of bad news, there were no outbursts from Cassie that afternoon.

Flushing

"Flushing" is used to deal with double messages; it involves responding literally to what the sender *says* rather than to what you're pretty sure she *means*. One example of this tactic was given earlier. When someone transmits a double message—sending nonverbal signals that contradict her words—generally make one or two sincere attempts to metacommunicate, gently acknowledging both sides of the message and inviting the controller to discuss the matter. If the controller persists in denying the nonverbal signals she is sending, simply ignore the nonverbals, and respond literally to the verbal message. For instance:

MELINDA: ". . . and I'm *not* angry!

HOOVER: Look, I hear you saying that you aren't angry. But when I see you glaring at me, slamming cabinet doors, and pacing around, I can't help thinking there's something wrong. If something's bothering you, I wish you would tell me about it.

MELINDA: I'm not angry! Nothing's bothering me! And I wish *you'd* stop telling *me* how I feel!

HOOVER: You're right. I shouldn't make assumptions about your feelings. I'm glad nothing's bothering you. I'm going to go watch TV. Want to join me?

MELINDA: No!

HOOVER: Okay. See you later.

Then, no matter how many nonverbal signals to the contrary he picks up, unless she tells him otherwise (or changes tactics), Hoover acts as if his wife is not angry. If he stands firm in spite of the emotional turmoil Melinda's nonverbal signals create, she will eventually realize that she is not getting the response she wants and may try something else.

Flushing is no panacea, and Melinda may never become particularly easy to live with. Pouters, deniers, and other controllers who use combinations of emotional exploitation and disconnection tactics are traditionally very difficult to influence. In this case, Melinda may well escalate her attempt to control, and Hoover will then have to deal with a new control tactic and the emotional uproar it causes.

This variation of the flushing maneuver is best used as a last resort and only if you are willing to use it consistently, and deal with the negative short-term consequences that may result. On the plus side, if you do use it and stick to your guns, there is a good chance that ultimately the controller will send you fewer double messages—simply because they are not working anymore.

Firing the Messenger

"Third-party referencing" is a control tactic in which the controller attributes a feeling, opinion or demand to someone else (for example, "I don't have a problem with the contract, but Bill won't sign it until you make these eight changes"). No matter how suspicious you are, the first time someone uses third-party referencing on you, take the message at face value—but also gently set limits on the behavior. ("Thanks for conveying Bill's position to me. I'll take a look at those clauses right away. But I have a request. I'd prefer that you don't do Bill's dirty work for him in the future. I'll be more than happy to talk to him myself.")

The next time the "messenger" makes this move (and since it worked the last time, you can rest assured he'll use it again), thank him for delivering the message and assure him that you'll take care of the matter as soon as you hear from the third party ("I'm glad you made me aware of Bill's new concern. Let him know that I'm waiting to hear from him so we can discuss it"). Since the controller knows you won't be hearing from the third party, he may decide to be more direct with you about his own concerns, and you can begin to deal with them.

When the controller uses third-party referencing to avoid owning up to his own feelings, you can try a gentle version of the flushing technique:

FATHER: I can understand why you want to live with your boyfriend, but your mother was devastated by the news.

DAUGHTER: I'm glad *you* don't feel that way. I'll call Mom and talk to her about it right away.

If Mom isn't being quoted accurately, Dad may stop his daughter from making the call and admit that he has some strong feelings about her decision himself.

Countering Deception Tactics

Deception is a particularly difficult maneuver to deal with. Until the same person has taken you in you several times, you have no good way of knowing *beforehand* that you are probably going to be deceived. Afterward, of course, it's too late. Also, skilled controllers only deceive you some of the time. Mostly they are being honest with you, and if you accuse them of dishonesty *then*, righteous indignation will flow like water. Even if they are deceiving you, confronting them with their dishonesty is apt to be pointless. They will simply try to deceive you once more by denying that they were deceiving you in the first place. Consequently, the best way to proceed is to take into account their past track record, assume that under certain circumstances they will lie to you, and cover yourself accordingly.

However, there is something specific you should *not* do. *Don't make verbal agreements with people who you know break verbal agreements!* This sounds like elementary advice, but in fact many of us do it all the time. And we have the funniest way of explaining why we did it:

JOAN: Why in the world did you expect him to call if he hasn't called the last seven times running?

BARB: I don't know. He's thirty-seven years old and he promised he'd call *for sure* this time. He knows how worried I get. Don't you think I should be able to trust him?

JOAN: So you expected him to do what he *should* do, rather than what he's *done* for the past two years! Does that seem very smart to you?

BARB: Well, I thought maybe this time would be different.

JOAN: Right.

The rule with agreement-breakers is *Get it in writing.* At work, that's often easy—the hard part is getting yourself to do it. Immediately after making a new agreement (with someone who broke a prior one), send a confirming memo. And if it's appropri-

199

ate within your company, send a copy to his boss. If memos don't work, keep dated notes detailing the agreement. At least this will keep you from doubting yourself when the controller comes in next week and says, "You're dreaming, I never agreed to . . ." Also, if things escalate, those notes might come in handy with the boss—or even in a court of law.

At home it can be trickier. You can certainly still take notes to keep yourself on track. You can be doggedly unwilling to accept broken agreements, bringing them up time after time. You can use the DESC model or a variation to try to get your message across as clearly as possible. Most of all, you can be discriminating about whom you make verbal agreements with; and with the agreements you do make, be even more discriminating about the ones on which you actually rely.

200

Follow-up

These advanced "verbal aikido" techniques are powerful, and they work. But remember this: no aikido player would *ever* take one lesson or read one book, and then assume he could defend himself if attacked on the street. Aikido takes practice, and so does good communication—especially if you're intending to use it with a control freak who, up till now, has pretty much been able to have his way with you. In the heat of battle, you will find yourself defaulting to your old patterns unless you've learned these new alternatives very, very well indeed.

Though you can practice on your own, it works best to find a friend who would also like to know the material. Then role-play *a lot*, until the new tactics begin to become second nature to you.

Better yet, return to Chapter 6 and design a series of modular reprogramming exercises to help you practice specific tactics under high-pressure conditions. Work with your partner as Lisa worked with Tracy. Eventually, the new moves will begin to be there for you, when, as, and if you need them. Then you'll be ready to use them with real control freaks, and in real-life situations.

CHAPTER
9

INTEGRATION
TAKING IT BACK TO THE REAL WORLD

Reading about effective methods for dealing with control freaks is one thing; applying those methods under pressure and with an actual person is something else again. Whether you learn a new skill from a book, a seminar, or the newest audiotape series on how to be a Really Terrific Person, taking that skill home and using it in the real world is *tough*. The real world can be a dangerous, lonely and uncaring place. It contains control freaks in abundance, and some of them will *never* be on your team. The truth is, sometimes it's much more comfortable to choose a familiar road you know leads nowhere than to risk traveling an unfamiliar one that could take you where you want to go.

Still, there are people who do have the resolve, courage and tenacity it takes to make some real changes. The last couple of chapters in this book will never be mistaken for casual reading; so if you've made it this far, it is fair to assume you might be one of them. Welcome to the unfamiliar road. I hope you'll find that what you've read has provided some groundwork and a useful beginning for your journey. Here are a few more thoughts and reminders to help you on your way.

Your Main Goal Shouldn't Be to Change the Control Freak

It is extremely hard to beat people at their own game, especially if it's not even a game you particularly like playing. Instead, work toward making changes in *yourself* that will leave you less vulnerable to control maneuvers and more able to respond effectively when called upon to do so. This approach takes skill, courage and dedication, but you can do it if you want to. Of course, the changes you make in yourself may, in turn, have a strong influence on the people around you. The control freak in your life really may change as well. If so, congratulations. But don't *expect* him or her to change, except very slowly and gradually over time.

Take Care You Don't Become a Control Freak Yourself

When you look closely, the differences between control freaks, accommodators and the rest of us begin to get a little hazy. We all play various roles in our lives; and there is a little of both the accommodator and the control freak in everyone. In some relationships, who is doing what to whom at any particular time is more a matter of perspective and personal bias than anything else.

In any case, the methods presented in Chapters 6 to 8 are powerful, and they work. Use that power wisely! Many of the advanced tactics presented in Chapter 8 could be used just as easily to control as to redirect or collaborate. Please don't use this book as a way to become a more effective control freak!

By the same token, take care not to use the techniques you learned here in an insincere or perfunctory manner, or without an honest intent to communicate. The aikido alternative really has very little to do with techniques—techniques just happen to be the tools you use to get the job done. *Used without integrity, they are hollow shells, and in the long run can be extremely destructive.* Here is an example.

Philip was a very successful executive whose wife, Jane, was upset because he seemed to care so much more about his work than he did about her. When she told him this, Philip duly professed his love, and then asked her what he could possibly have done to give her such a crazy notion. Among other things, Jane told him he never sent her flowers anymore; it meant to her that the romance had gone out of their relationship, that he no longer cared.

The next day, Jane received a very attractive flower arrangement, and was so happy she nearly cried. Of course, it wasn't the flowers themselves that were important to her as much as the fact that Philip had finally understood, and had responded so quickly. Maybe he cared after all. From then on, Jane received flowers from her husband every week (always on Thursday morning), and began to feel just a little like she had when she and Philip were courting. That is, until, while paying bills at the end of the month, she came across an invoice from the *flower service* Philip had retained to see that his wife got her weekly dose of romance.

Some people find this story appalling. A few don't believe it really happened—they laugh and say, "Come on, you just made that up to underscore your point about hollow techniques." (And others think for a moment, then shrug and say, "Sounds ok to me. Responsive, efficient, the wife got her flowers—but why didn't Philip just have the flower service bill him at the office?)

This incident really happened. And, although most of us don't put our spouses on flower services, in smaller ways we do similar kinds of things. When we say, "Yes, dear . . ." without really listening, listen without really hearing, or use any technique in a hollow, insincere manner, we are putting the other person on a kind of "communication service." While this may work for a while, in the long run it will be just as destructive as Philip's little time-saver was to his marriage.

203

Don't Expect to Win Them All

Most negotiations with serious control freaks fall into the "low-probability outcome" category. Even when conditions are ideal and you do everything right, you'll probably lose a lot more frequently than you'll win. Don't let that stop you, and whatever happens, don't evaluate the quality of your performance on the basis of whether or not you achieved the outcome you wanted. Instead, judge it in terms of the extent to which you were able to *take your best shot.* For instance, assume that under ideal conditions your chances of winning a particular point were one in five. Did you give yourself the full benefit of that 20 percent? Or did you get discouraged partway through because you "probably weren't going to succeed anyway," and not try very hard, thereby reducing your actual chances from 20 percent to 5 or 10 percent?

Anything That's Worth Doing Is Worth Doing Badly

This was said earlier, but it bears repeating. The only way you'll ever learn to do anything well is to give yourself permission to make mistakes and to look and sound clumsy when you're starting out. Most people accept that, when they're learning to ski or ride a bicycle. But communication is a little different. It's *embarrassing* to sound clumsy or uncertain. Yet, being able to stumble around and sound weird for a while is a critically important part of the learning process. Give yourself permission to do so. Skills you learn at a seminar or from a self-help book will wear off if you don't practice them. It would be a shame if that happened to you because you were concerned about what other people might think if you did something wrong.

Here is an anticipation tactic sometimes given to workshop participants who would like to use their new skills on the job, but are concerned that the boss might criticize or misjudge this learning-phase clumsiness.

The participant is instructed to meet with his or her boss soon after returning from the seminar, and say something like "Thanks for sending me to that class. It was a valuable experience, and I think the company will get its investment back in spades. I'm going to start using the skills I learned there immediately. So if I sound or act a little strange over the next few days, please cut me some slack. This stuff is still new to me, and I may not be very good at it yet. But we invested good time and money in that seminar; I want to make sure I practice until I get everything down pat." In most cases, not only will the boss cut his employee some slack, but he will express sincere appreciation for the extra effort. And, of course, the employee now has permission to make some mistakes.

See if you can come up with a variation on this theme that will give *you* permission to "do it badly" for a while as you practice your newfound skills.

"Be Like the Water, Not the Rock"

This ancient Japanese proverb refers to the effect water has as it runs down a rocky streambed. The rocks stand firm and impenetrable while the water yields, changing direction and flowing around the rocks in order to continue downhill. But come back in three or four hundred years, and things have changed: those majestic, impenetrable rocks are nowhere to be found! They have been worn away, while the water peacefully flows on.

Patience and persistence are cornerstones of the aikido alternative. Most fights aren't decided by one punch, and most control issues are not decided in one sitting. If you don't seem to be making much headway with your controller, don't panic. Stay with it. Do switch methods if you think the one you're using is ineffective, but continue to persevere. Be patient. Allow enough time for the full effects of your alignment and redirection tactics to develop.

In some cases, things may get worse for a while before they get better. That is, the controller may become angrier, more stubborn, or may try even harder to control you. This is usually a sign that your efforts are beginning to have an effect: stay with it. Remember the "net model" presented in Chapter 6: cut one interlacing at a time. Eventually the net will become weaker, and you may well break free.

What to Do if Nothing Works

Or you may not. Unfortunately, there are people around, who will continue to try to control you no matter what you do. Some may be able to short-circuit you successfully because you need a job, have children to think of, or don't think you can make it on your own. Others will be able to manipulate you simply because you love them. They won't think twice about using your love against you, and won't feel the slightest twinge of guilt about it afterward.

Everything that's been said so far still goes. But as you continue working, also keep one eye on what your relationship with the control freak is costing you. When the relationship begins to cost you more than you get back in return—and when it's pretty clear nothing is going to change—then it may be time for you to decide whether to stay or to go.

Making the Choice

This kind of choice can be extremely difficult and painful; usually there are no easy answers. Sometimes, in our hearts, we know we should end a marriage, change jobs, terminate a friendship, or fire a pleasant, hardworking, but terminally incompetent employee. But the practical and/or emotional consequences of doing so would be devastating. So we stay in the relationship, keep the job, retain the employee—and then spend half our waking hours moaning about the trouble and pain the relationship is continuing to cause. We alternate between hating the other person for creating so much misery, and hating ourselves for being so weak.

It's beyond the scope of this book to deal with such choices. Keeping a diary, attending a support group, delving into the self-help literature, speaking with a trusted friend, a minister, a counselor or therapist—all of these might help. On the other hand, sometimes nothing helps. Friends, spiritual beliefs, professional counseling and other resources can be tremendously valuable. But, ultimately, the decision, the responsibility for the consequences of making that decision, and all the accompanying doubt and pain are yours to bear.

Furthermore, no matter how many resources you have, and no matter how hard you work with them, you'll almost certainly never have enough information to make a truly "rational" decision. You'll remain unsure, you'll be shooting in the dark. And, no matter what choice you make, a part of you will be certain that it was the wrong one. Yet continuing to avoid the issue makes matters worse. Only by confronting the problem and doing something about it can you ever hope to be free.

Reasons You Might Choose Not to End a Relationship . . . Yet

- You could lose your job and have trouble finding another or surviving without a paycheck until you do.

- You are not willing or emotionally prepared to go through a divorce or end a relationship.

- The control freak is prone to violence and you know from past experience that resisting his control or upsetting the status quo sets him off.

- Control freak is emotionally unstable, severely depressed, mourning a loss, an alcoholic or addict in the early stages of recovery, or under a great deal of stress; and you have reason to believe that changing the way you relate to her now would push her over the edge.

- For the time being, you simply cannot handle one additional major source of stress in your life—you're stretched nearly to the breaking point as it is.

- The control freak is your parent or someone else with whom you've had a long-standing relationship. You know that even redefining the relationship is unlikely to change anything and doesn't seem worth the uproar it will cause.

- The other person's controlling behavior is the only major flaw in an otherwise satisfying relationship or work situation. On balance, you're willing to accept the bad with the good.

207

Sometimes, only one practical alternative is available to you: you *must* remain in the relationship because circumstances force you to do so. For instance, Barbara, the single mother who worked for a chauvinistic boss (page 35), had no immediate option but to continue at her job despite the indignities she suffered there. What about people like Barbara? If you have only one option available, can you still *choose* that option? Or are you forced into it, doing what you do simply because you "have no choice"?

Philosophically, this is a debatable point. But from a practical standpoint the answer is clear: *it's up to you!* You can play the trapped and unfortunate victim of circumstances, resentful, resistant and suffering. Or you can *freely choose the lone option available* to you, your head high, on the lookout for lemons from which to squeeze some lemonade.

This isn't just a matter of positive thinking and being a good sport. You aren't just making do or kidding yourself into feeling better. Rather, you are like the aikido player who has lost the advantage to his opponent and is about to be thrown to the mat. Ideally, the aikidoist might prefer to be doing the throwing, but that isn't how things worked out. So, rather than wasting time on might-have-beens, he "goes with the flow" and *chooses to be thrown.*

Now the aikido player tries to be a perfectly balanced and focused "throwee." Not only does he offer no resistance to his opponent, he actually assists him in executing the throw. In doing so he retains some control over what's happening and can partially redirect the energies involved in the movement. Almost literally "riding the tiger in the direction it's going," he flies through the air, lands exactly as he planned to, and quickly rolls to his feet. He is centered, balanced, focused and immediately ready to continue the contest—very possibly more ready than his opponent, who has expected to find a thrown and momentarily helpless adversary lying on the mat.

Did the aikido player really choose to be thrown, or did he have no choice? From a practical standpoint, it doesn't really matter. The choices he did make gave him tremendous power and control *even though he still got thrown!* You can learn to make the same kinds of choices—and as a result, have available to you at least some of the same kind of power.

208

If You Choose to Stay

Let's return to Barbara. By and large she likes her job, she gets to work flextime when necessary to deal with baby-sitting problems, and the fact is she'd probably have to take a pay cut if she left her current situation. She is saving what little she can for an eventual return to school, and certainly doesn't want to reduce her income unless absolutely necessary. On the other hand Barbara's boss, Tony, calls her "honey," can be just a bit too free with his hands, and apparently thinks women were born to fetch coffee and make babies. In addition, he regularly asks Barbara to dinner, despite clear signals (according to Barbara) that she has no interest in pursuing a social relationship.

"You just can't imagine how much I resent it!" she continued. "I'm nice to Tony because I have to be, but every time he puts his hand on my arm during a conversation and I don't spit on it, I feel like a whore. What a slimeball he is."

"Have you ever asked him not to touch you?"

"A couple of times. Oh, he takes his hand away, but he makes some stupid joke about how sensitive I am. Then a few days later he's back at it. That kind of thing really embarrasses me. I guess I'm just not very assertive."

Barbara said she liked most of the other people at work, and didn't want to rock the boat by lodging a formal complaint. She just wanted the problem to go away. She resented the situation, hated herself for not being more forceful with Tony, and had ruined many an afternoon alternately fuming over the last time Tony cooed, "Honey, could you run me in some coffee, there's a good girl," and worrying about what she'd say if Tony asked her out again that evening.

Writing It into Your Job Description Basically, Barbara was playing victim, and needed help to take a different approach. As much of an insensitive chauvinist as her boss might be (and none of the following should be construed as an attempt to let Tony off the hook), most of the frustration, helplessness, and self-contempt she felt as a result of his actions was created by Barbara herself.

I asked Barbara if she would be willing to actively and freely *choose* to work for Tony, chauvinism, slime and all. When she indignantly said no, I reminded her that every morning she gets out of bed, brushes her teeth, and essentially does just that.

"But I have no choice! I need the money!" she replied, a little angrily.

"That's not true. If it were important enough to you, there are a lot of other things you could do."

Now Barbara was steaming. "But Tony has no *right* to treat me the way he does!"

"You're absolutely correct—Tony is way out of line. But so what? You either can't or won't do anything about it. He sure isn't going to change on his own, and the Masked Crusader isn't due for weeks. That's just the way it is.

"Now, if you 'choose' to work for Tony," I went on, "you'll get up tomorrow morning, go to work, and maybe get slimed by him a couple of times. On the other hand, if you continue to resent the hell out of the whole arrangement, tell yourself how unfair it all is, and work for him tomorrow only because you have to, you'll get up, go to the office, and maybe get slimed by him a couple of times. Seems like it comes out about the same either way, doesn't it? You can hang on to your 'helpless victim' perspective if it's that important to you. But you really have nothing to lose by trying something a little different."

After a few more stories about steering in the direction of the skid, aikido players choosing to be thrown, and so on, Barbara

209

agreed to "choose" to work for Tony. "But how do I do that?" she asked.

Barbara was instructed to go home that night and *write out a detailed job description*—including duties, salary level, perks, everything. In it she was to emphasize the parts of the job that involved working for Tony—not the Tony that *should* exist, the Tony that really did exist.

For instance, one of her items read, "I'm getting paid $15.25 per hour to work for a boss who calls me 'honey' and touches me when he talks." Another read, "I'm being paid a salary plus unofficial flextime to put up with an insensitive boss who clearly can't take a hint."

"So," I asked her when she brought her new job description back to the office, "is this a pretty accurate description of what goes on at work, and what you get in exchange?"

"It sure is!" she said, "But it shouldn't be this way!"

"Maybe not, but—"

"I know, 'that's just the way it is,' " she replied, finishing my sentence for me.

"Right. So do you accept the assignment? Knowing what to expect, having the benefit of full disclosure beforehand? Freely? No resentment? Payment for services rendered? A straightforward business contract?"

"I guess so," she said, smiling a little at my formality and mock severity.

"Good. Then, the next time Tony comes over and slimes on you, you don't have to like it, you can even give him a hard time about it if you want to. But *don't take it personally!* It's just a part of your business contract. Comes with the territory. It doesn't mean he's taking advantage of you, or that you're compromising yourself, or anything else. It's business. Just relax, take a breath, and say to yourself, 'I'm being paid $15.25 per hour to put up with a sexist boss with the sensitivity of a radish.' It's *just business.*"

"But does this mean I'll have to put up with this kind of treatment for the rest of my life?"

"You were putting up with it to begin with, and then making yourself miserable to boot. But we'll let that go. No, it doesn't. Quite the contrary. This will help you stop hating yourself and ruining your afternoons worrying about how you're being treated. Now, if you'd also like to *change* the way you're being treated, great! Let's talk about that."

INTEGRATION

Barbara and I discussed the issue of assertiveness. She agreed that she could use some work in that area, and allowed that Tony probably wouldn't fire her if she were more assertive with him. "Actually, in a way he might like it; I know it would make me a better employee. He really isn't *quite* the slimeball I've been making him out to be. I'm just so darn sensitive to him."

Barbara agreed to add the following line to her new job description: "One of my projects over the next ninety days is to develop the following assertion skills [we made a list of very basic skills] and use them with Tony. The project deadline is [date], and my specific performance objectives are [she listed several observable goals]."

Over the next few months, Barbara did learn to take Tony's behavior less personally. She successfully completed an assertion training class. Gradually, she developed the ability to maintain eye contact with Tony, ask him to keep his hands to himself when necessary, and to refuse dinner invitations she didn't want to accept.

On his part, Tony never did change much. He remained the insensitive, rather boorish (though basically well-meaning) chauvinist he'd always been. But after a while, Barbara simply wasn't much bothered by it. She had really "written him into her job description"—had learned to accept him for what he was and not allow him to reduce the quality of her life. In turn, the relief and confidence this provided allowed her to go further, changing her behavior in ways she'd never before been able to do. And gradually, because she wasn't such an easy target anymore, Tony began to back off.

To summarize: Consciously choose your course of action, even when you really have only one alternative available. Taking responsibility for that choice will help you adopt a proactive stance rather than acting like a helpless victim. Accept, rather than resent or resist, those problems you can't change. *Write them into your job description.* Then work with the parts of the situation you *can* do something about. Who knows, things may get better. Or your circumstances may change in a way that will allow you to consider another alternative: dissolving the relationship once and for all.

If You Choose to Leave

When Kim returned to college, she made several eye-opening discoveries. She realized she was not as dumb as she'd originally thought or as Alan had led her to believe. She learned that people could like and even look up to her as she was—no molding, shaping or special instructions needed! Her self-esteem and self-confidence grew by leaps and bounds. Naïvely, Kim expected Alan to be pleased by these changes. Guess what?

"The way he acted you would have thought I was seeing another guy or something," Kim said. "He set up this competition. If he could get me to pay attention to him instead of my schoolwork or my school friends, he won. And you know Alan, he hates to lose. The first semester I was in school, he was more demanding and controlling than he'd ever been before."

Alan tried every trick in the book to undermine Kim's confidence and bring her back under his control. She used the aikido strategies she had learned at a weekend seminar, but had only limited success with them. "He just switched tactics," Kim said. "If I convinced him not to ask me for suggestions and then ridicule them, he'd make plans that conflicted with my schedule and would say that I'd told him not to consult me. He stopped badgering me about doing things with him when I had to study. He tried to seduce or bribe me instead. It was absolutely endless."

Concluding that her life would be less stressful if she just gave in to Alan and accommodated him in any way she could, during her second semester Kim resumed her peacemaking patterns. "Alan was thrilled," Kim said. "But I was miserable."

Kim was caught between the old and the new. Flattering, placating, stifling her true feelings, and smoothing over all conflicts were not automatic behaviors anymore. Kim was consciously aware of what she was doing and had a hard time justifying it to herself, much less anyone else. "My school friends couldn't believe what I put up with. They kept asking me why I let Alan treat me the way he did and after a while, listening to what I told them made *me* gag."

When Kim began to notice that she felt panicky and got migraine headaches before and during her visits with Alan and felt relieved and relaxed when she was away from him, she finally realized that it was time to throw in the towel.

Kim ended her relationship with Alan about a year ago. Currently she is applying to graduate school and is romantically involved with a man she described as "nothing like Alan. He'll never earn as much money, never rub elbows with the rich and famous, never know as much about fine wine," she said. "But he's easy-going and understanding and exactly what I need."

Making the Break   As Kim discovered, some people are not about to change and will persistently make you pay for changing yourself in any way. If that description fits the control freak in your life and you have reached a point where you are no longer receiving enough benefits to warrant putting up with that person, it's time to start thinking about changing your situation or getting out of it altogether.

That option has always been available to you, but for one reason or another, you have postponed considering or pursuing it. Quitting a job, ending a relationship, even cutting down on the contact you have with your controlling mother or spending less time with a controlling friend is not something to be taken lightly or done hastily. However, when all other options have been exhausted, when *you* are exhausted from trying them and when—despite your best efforts—matters have gotten progressively worse, *then* walking away from the situation can move to the top of your options list.

213

Of course, you don't want to just bolt for the nearest door. Don't act first and think later. You need an escape plan.

Step One: Assign a specific period of time to make one last effort to resolve the problem without leaving. Try any options you may have previously shunned—most notably getting outside help. Depending on what you are hoping to accomplish, allot a week, a month or more for this purpose. Make an honest effort and give this final try your best shot; but if you haven't seen positive results by your deadline, it's time to move on. If things get bad enough, of course, you can quit sooner. On the other hand, if your situation does begin to change for the better, feel free to extend the deadline.

Step Two: Make sure you have somewhere to escape *to*— another job lined up or enough money saved to support yourself while you look; a place to live if you must leave your current residence; child care if you'll have to work outside your home; a divorce lawyer; a restraining order—in other words, whatever it will take to make a smoother transition, including a source of emotional support.

Step Three: Determine exactly how you are going to make the break, when you are going to inform the control freak of your decision, even what you want to say. You may want to rehearse with a friend. Try to cover all contingencies, including the possibility of delaying your getaway should unforseen circumstances arise.

Step Four: Carry out your plan. Be aware that wherever you go, you take yourself with you. If you still see yourself as a powerless victim and present yourself to the world in a manner that gets other people to see you that way too, you will continue to be victimized. If you are still driven to people-please or sacrifice yourself for the greater good of others, you will continue to find yourself in situations that require you to do just that. And if you are still walking around with your dukes up or carrying around a suitcase full of resentments, you will find new adversaries around every bend. Changing your situation will *not* change your life unless you also gain new insight, new awareness and new skills, and use them to change yourself.

214

Getting Additional Help

Now and then we all have trouble seeing the forest for the trees. We can run around in the same circle for years, missing the turnoff time after time or never realizing that there are other roads to take. Sometimes we are too close to the control freak or too entangled in a control trap to identify our part in it objectively or figure out what to do about it. Few of us can break lifelong habits or change long-standing patterns on our own. Fortunately, there are people and resources to help us stop spinning our wheels and start moving forward again.

Professional Help

If you are having trouble extracting yourself from a control trap or want to make sure you don't get caught in another one anytime soon, consider taking advantage of one or more of the following sources of outside help.

Individual therapy offers you one-on-one attention from a trained helping professional—a psychiatrist, psychologist, social worker or counselor. Therapy is particularly useful for uncovering your old programming and removing barriers to change. By getting to the bottom of your negative behavior patterns, you improve your chances of breaking old habits and replacing them with more effective coping strategies.

Just as you won't get along with everyone you meet, you won't necessarily be helped by every therapist listed in the telephone book. Therapists have different styles, different types of training and different specialties that affect their approach to treating patients. As a result, the first professional you consult may not be able to supply the kind of help you need. Recognizing that your own fears about being in therapy may be getting in your way, try to give the therapist time to help you. If, after several therapy sessions, you still feel that you are not being helped, tell that to your therapist, clearly stating what is bothering you and what you would like to be different. A reputable therapist will hear you out and either try to meet your needs or refer you to another therapist. You have the right to part company with any therapist who is not helping you—*especially* one who gives you a hard time for saying so.

215

Couples therapy helps identify the attitudes, behaviors and communication problems that are getting and keeping you stuck in a control trap within a relationship. Strengthening your relationship and getting both of you to adopt new, mutually satisfying ways of relating to each other is the goal. However, couples therapy is *not* designed to keep two people together at any cost. In fact, you and your partner may decide that no matter how much either of you changes, the relationship still will not work. By coming to this conclusion in therapy rather than without it, you will be able to walk away with more peace of mind and be less likely to repeat your control patterns in your next relationship.

Group therapy offers you a safe place to practice new communication skills and reprogram yourself. With a therapist overseeing the interaction between group members, you can take risks and relate to other people in new ways. Useful, eye-opening insights come from both group members and group leaders, who give practical suggestions that can help you learn to assert yourself, revise negative self-talk, test out your theories about your effect on other people, and discuss and rehearse upcoming interactions. You will also receive feedback that can help you fine-tune your approach to dealing with the controlling people in your life.

Family therapy involves treating the family unit as the patient so that all members can work together to improve relationships and communication. This approach prevents unhealthy habits from being passed on to the next generation and stops family members from unwittingly supporting one another's controlling or accommodating behavior.

Self-help and Support Groups

Self-help and peer support groups are excellent resources for relieving your sense of isolation, giving you a new perspective on your problems, helping you develop self-confidence, and improving your communication skills. The process of helping yourself while helping other people has proven so effective that support groups for victims of abuse, victimizers, widows and widowers, divorcés, adult children of alcoholics, families of the mentally ill and almost any other population imaginable exist in most communities. We don't know of any support groups for people involved with control freaks but if you have one of the above problems, those groups can help you with your control problems too. Another possibility, and one which you should consider seriously, is to start your own support group. You'd be surprised how many of your friends, neighbors and colleagues might voice real interest—but would never have suggested the idea on their own.

Workshops and Seminars

The more communication skills you develop and the more you learn about yourself and other people, the better equipped you will be to handle whatever the controlling people in your life throw at you. Seminars, weekend workshops and ongoing courses that teach communication skills, assertiveness, stress reduction, time management or visualization techniques can be particularly helpful. Marriage encounter weekends and couples communication courses can strengthen a relationship that has been damaged by conflicts and power struggles. Workshops and courses in your area may be organized or sponsored by churches, community colleges, adult education programs, singles organizations, mental health clinics and men's, women's or couples' resource centers. Check them out.

216

Aikido Instruction

Aikido *dojos* exist in nearly every large American city. Drop in some evening and get a feeling for what aikido training is all about. *Dojos* nearly always welcome unannounced visitors; you will be able to observe a training session and possibly a demonstration by advanced students or instructors. The *sensei* (teacher) will be glad to answer any questions you might have.

Group lessons in the martial arts are generally quite inexpensive. Depending on the *dojo*, lessons are usually held several times a week. Students pay by the week or month, and for that fee may attend as many or as few sessions as they wish. In addition, some *dojos* offer introductory training packages.

Don't let a physical or medical problem stop you from exploring this variation of the aikido alternative. Unlike many other disciplines, aikido training stresses mental and spiritual development as much or more than physical self defense. In some *dojos*, the rolls and throws one normally associates with the martial arts play but a minor role in the training regimen.

217

Holding with an Open Hand: Reprise

We have covered a lot of territory together; now it's time to move on. I hope these pages have provided you with some useful alternatives, and that they work for you in the ways you want them to. But please remember the Law of Requisite Variety: the more options and alternatives you have, the better off you are. There are no "right answers," no "truths." There are only possibilities, and nothing is right for everyone. I ask that you hold the ideas you may have found here the way that boy learned to hold the little sparrow: with an open hand. Think about them, practice them, use them—then open your hand and make room for other ideas, other possibilities. The ones you wish to retain and continue to use will still be there for you when you need them.

Our journey together ends here, but the Journey never ends. I wish you well.

APPENDIX

SUGGESTED READING

This list of suggested readings contains some of the books I've found most useful. However, the list necessarily reflects my own biases, and a great many extremely valuable resources are not included. Check the sections devoted to addictions, self-help, psychology, or inspiration in any good library or bookstore.

Bandler, Richard, and John Grinder. *The Structure of Magic, Vol. I.* Cupertino, Calif.: Science and Behavior Books, 1975.

Beattie, Melody. *Codependent No More: How to Stop Controlling Others and Start Caring for Yourself.* New York: Harper & Row, 1987.

Beck, Aaron T. *Love Is Not Enough.* New York: Harper & Row, 1988.

Berne, Eric. *Games People Play.* New York: Dell, 1964.

Bower, Sharon A., and Gordon Bower. *Asserting Yourself: A Practical Guide for Positive Change.* New York: Addison-Wesley, 1976.

Brown, Stephanie. *Safe Passage: Recovery for Adult Children of Alcoholics.* New York: Wiley, 1991.

Campbell, Susan M. *Beyond the Power Struggle: Dealing with Conflict in Love and Work.* San Luis Obispo, Calif.: Impact Publishers, 1984.

Cohen, Herb. *You Can Negotiate Anything.* New York: Lyle Stuart, 1980.

Dobson, Terry, and Viktor Miller. *Giving In To Get Your Way.* New York: Delacorte, 1978.

Elgin, Suzette Haden. *Success with the Gentle Art of Verbal Self-Defense.* Englewood Cliffs, N.J.: Prentice-Hall, 1989.

Ellis, Albert. *How to Live with a Neurotic.* New York: Crown, 1975.

Ekman, Paul. *Telling Lies: Clues to Deceit in the Marketplace, Politics, and Marriage.* New York: Norton, 1985.

Fay, Allen. *PQR: Prescriptions for a Quality Relationship.* New York: Simon & Schuster, 1990.

Gendlin, Eugene T. *Focusing.* New York: Everest House, 1978.

Glasser, William. *Control Theory.* New York: Harper & Row, 1984.

Haley, J. *The Power Tactics of Jesus Christ and Other Essays, 2nd ed.* Rockville, Md.: Triangle Press, 1986.

Hayakawa, S.I. *Language in Thought and Action.* New York: Harcourt, 1964.

Keyes, Ken. *Handbook to Higher Consciousness.* Marina del Rey, Calif.: Living Love Publications, 1980.

Jacubowski, Patricia, and Arthur J. Lange. *The Assertive Option.* Champaign, Ill: Research Press, 1978.

Lazarus, Arnold A. *Marital Myths.* San Luis Obispo, Calif.: Impact Publishers, 1986.

Leonard, George. *The Ultimate Athlete.* New York: Viking, 1975.

Meichenbaum, Donald. *Stress-Inoculation Training.* New York: Pergamon, 1985.

Musashi, Miyamoto. *A Book of Five Rings: The Real Art of Japanese Management.* New York: Bantam, 1982.

Piaget, Gerald W., and Barbara Binkley. *Overcoming Your Barriers: A Guide to Personal Reprogramming.* New York: Irvington, 1985.

———. *How to Communicate Under Pressure: Dealing Effectively with Difficult People.* Portola Valley, Calif.: IAHB Press, 1985.

Richardson, Jerry, and Joel Margulis. *The Magic of Rapport.* San Francisco: Harbor Publishing, 1981.

SUGGESTED READING

Rogers, David J. *Fighting to Win: Samurai Techniques for Your Work and Life.* New York: Doubleday, 1984.

Rossman, Martin. *Healing Yourself: A Step-by-Step Program for Better Health Through Imagery.* New York: Walker, 1987.

Shostrum, Everett L. *Man, the Manipulator.* New York: Bantam, 1968.

Westbrook, A. M., and O. Rotti. *Aikido and the Dynamic Sphere.* Rutland, Vt.: Charles E. Tuttle, 1970.

INDEX

INDEX